GLUTTONY,
PRIDE AND LUST

and other sins
from the world of books

GLUTTONY, PRIDE AND LUST

and other sins
from the world of books

compiled and introduced by
MICHAEL TURNER
and **MICHAEL GEARE**
with a foreword by
HAROLD MACMILLAN
Illustrations by Val Biro

COLLINS
8 Grafton Street, London W1
1984

William Collins Sons & Co. Ltd
London · Glasgow · Sydney · Auckland
Toronto · Johannesburg

First published 1984
Copyright © Michael Turner and Michael Geare 1984

ISBN 0 00 216621 6

Photoset in Linotron Sabon by
Rowland Phototypesetting Ltd,
Bury St Edmunds, Suffolk
Made and printed in Great Britain by
T. J. Press (Padstow) Ltd., Padstow, Cornwall

'Now, Barabbas was a publisher'
Thomas Campbell

CONTENTS

FOREWORD

Compared to my colleagues and adversaries in the world of politics, I have found a book men and women to be more sinned against than sinning. I have always felt that their offences were more venial than mortal, and this charming and humorous collection proves that even in the case of gluttony the catalogue of bookish sins is really a pot-pourri of peccadilloes.

HAROLD MACMILLAN

INTRODUCTION

'PUBLISHERS ARE DEMONS,' said Henry James, 'there's no doubt about it.' And many of the stories we tell in this book prove just that. Legions of authors (up to and including Fay Weldon) have endorsed James's judgment, but that has not prevented countless fresh-faced, well-educated and idealistic young persons annually from seeking a job in publishing. There are many contradictions in this volume, but we have to be brave and admit that it confirms authors' worst fears.

Perhaps it all comes down to money. In 1812, Isaac Disraeli, father of Benjamin, published with the first John Murray a two-volume work entitled *Calamities of Authors*. He listed all kinds of disasters from melancholia to blindness, taking in critics on the way, but oddly enough publishers and booksellers were not among his major misfortunes. Disraeli, however, was little concerned with the business aspect of authorship. 'In commercial times,' he wrote, 'the hope of profit is always a stimulating but degrading motive; it dims the clearest intellect, it stills the proudest feelings.' This collection concentrates on that ignoble but fascinating trait: it is about people who make money from books without actually writing them.

Some of our stories go back several centuries, but most of our tales are about publishers in this century, largely British, many American, with a sprinkling from Australia, New Zealand and other places where they publish. If we have

found or been told good stories about those closely associated with publishers – booksellers, literary agents, reviewers, printers, even authors – we have joyfully included them.

A recent article in the American journal *Publishers Weekly*
observed that 'linguists once agreed that the phrase "publishing business" was an oxymoron [*PW* was too classy to
explain that this was a combination of contradictory terms]
similar to "American culture" or "army intelligence": in
those long-ago days BC (Before Conglomerates), people
entered the business more for the love of books than for the
love of bucks.' The evidence of the lives and characters of
the publishers as revealed in these pages, with a few notable
exceptions, shows the exact opposite. Indeed one can only
marvel at the sharpness of their business sense – to say
nothing of their business practice – and their love of bucks is
intense. It is hard to imagine a closer fraternity of tight-
wads.

There has been sufficient reason for this characteristic:
the urge to survive. Desmond Elliott told us that a maxim of
Jonathan Cape's has stayed with him throughout his business life: 'Publishing pays . . . if you don't charge for your
time.'

Another myth that here receives a rude setback is that of
the publisher as literary man, as distinct from a bookman.
Not only were many of our greatest publishers far from
literary; some were barely literate. Of course, there were
and are sensitive and immensely cultured people in the
trade, fit to be called literary publishers by any standards,
but they have seldom been the creators of great publishing
houses, let alone dynasties. One can name plenty of literary
publishers from Leonard Woolf to Tom Rosenthal to whom
British and American writing must ever be thereby in-
debted. But how many built firms that survived them?
Now the game of nomination becomes much more difficult.
As for the Longmans, Murrays, Scribners, Macmillans,

Doubledays, Dents, Methuens, Lippincotts and Unwins, they were men who knew the value of books and how they could be marshalled to make money, but were seldom the material for honorary D. Lits. It was John Murray who is supposed to have provoked the poet Thomas Campbell to observe that 'Barabbas was a publisher'. It has generally been only the descendants of these great businessmen who could afford to assume literary pretentions.

So, like Milton, we fell in love with Lucifer. There are many tales of kindly, responsive, generous bookmen – we include a touching example under the heading of Gluttony – but their good deeds have usually been performed surreptitiously. Book people are just as noble, and as base, as the rest of humanity, but this is a book designed as entertainment and we have to admit, alas, that for the compiler of anecdotes bad news is good news.

It is the *monstres sacrés* who dominate; between them they break all the Commandments except, possibly, the sixth, plus a few more that the Almighty might have encountered had he been directly involved in the publication of his works. The novelist and inveterate bookman, the late Frank Swinnerton, born in the 1880s and with publishing recollections stretching back over eighty years, told us that in his younger days 'all the publishers were ruffians'. We thought it appropriate to plan our collection to encompass the Seven Deadly Sins, but they turned out to be insufficiently comprehensive. We have therefore added one more, that sin so well known to the British Conservative Party, Being Found Out. Only a single virtue intrudes, and this we gladly concede to the business of books: Enterprise.

Prosper Merimée said, 'In history I love only anecdotes, and among anecdotes I prefer those where I think I can distinguish a true picture of the customs and characters of any given period.' We would go even further than Merimée. We are bold enough to think that in anecdotes we can

13

distinguish not only the characteristics of the time, but the characteristics of our business that transcend time – and also the kind of human beings involved. We suspect that even among the mud tablets of Ur thrived a Walter Hutchinson or a Charles Scribner.

Our stories come from a wide variety of sources. We do not claim them to be in any sense comprehensive; we rejected many and chose only those we most enjoyed. We have dipped with relish into histories, biographies and autobiographies. One lively set of memoirs in two volumes by the Victorian publisher, William Tinsley, we found on the shelves of the Publishers Association, the pages still uncut. We had splendid rambling conversations with such bookmen as Frank Swinnerton and the wickedly observant Clarence Paget, and with such bookish knights as Sir John Brown, Sir Robert Lusty and the late Sir Basil Blackwell.

A number of friends set pen to paper on our behalf, the most prolific among them being Lord Horder, Michael Rubinstein, Ian Norrie, Desmond Elliott and Ralph Vernon-Hunt. We thank them all, as we do the very large number of people who delighted us with tales old and new, generous and upon occasions scurrilous. As to their accuracy – well, see below. Our contributors include, in strict alphabetical order, Barley Allison, Neil Aston, Philip Attenborough, Ian Chapman, Charles Clark, Michael Corby, Robin Denniston, George Depotex, Margaret Drabble, Colin Eccleshare, Richard Findlater, Christopher Falkus, Roland Grant, Tom Hodges, Nic Jones, Michael Marland, Trevor Moore, John Murray, Eric Norris, Jim Reynolds, Ben Russak, Paul Scherer, Roger Schlesinger, David Whitaker and Len Woodley.

Many of our tales are undoubtedly apocryphal. That has not prevented us from reproducing them. Indeed, when we began to check their accuracy, the delightful fiction was sometimes replaced by much less colourful fact and we have shamelessly left some anecdotes unchecked. There is a story circulating about Sir Robert Lusty, a most distinguished publisher but undeniably a trifle hard of hearing, during his days at Hutchinson:

A young editor, it is said, rushed in one morning, newspaper in hand, to see him.

'R.L.,' he blurted out, 'Hitler's sister is writing her memoirs!'

'Where is she, James?'

'Berchtesgaden, R.L.'

'Then get after her, James. At once. Sign her up. If you want to be a real publisher you will have to move fast.'

The editor left the great man, exultant. *This* was publishing! He instructed his secretary to book a seat on the next flight to Munich, scheduled to leave at 4 pm. On his way out of the office at lunchtime, he bumped into Lusty.

'You still here, James? What are you waiting for? Didn't I tell you to get after Hitler's sister right away?'

'But, R.L., the next plane doesn't leave until four o'clock.'

A pause.

'*Where* did you say she lives?'

'Berchtesgaden.'

'My God, I thought you said Bedford Gardens.'

We thought it courteous to check the tale with Sir Robert. He recollected the incident, perfectly but quite differently. It was in fact the young editor who misheard: collapse of story. So, alerted to the danger of tarnishing some of our best gems we have not always sought corroboration of the facts. Some stories, therefore, may not be true, but we claim that even if they are not, they should be. They are the book trade's folk lore: usually a nugget of fact in a rich embroidered setting. Some well-known living figures appear in these dubious anecdotes and we may owe several full and comprehensive apologies: all we can say is that there is seldom so much smoke without at least a glimmer of fire.

We hope no one will issue a writ. We take comfort in the belief that as all proceeds from this book for both compilers and publishers are to be donated to Bookrest, the Book Trade Benevolent Society fund in Britain, there will be few so curmudgeonly as to seek to mulct a charity.

MICHAEL TURNER AND MICHAEL GEARE, 1984

LUST

THIS COLLECTION SHOWS how wholeheartedly book trade people embrace the Seven Deadly Sins. Lust, however, seems among the least pervasive; as compared, for example, with politicians, publishers appear as Mr and Ms Clean.

With inevitable exceptions – Sir Allen Lane and Horace Liveright are two of them – publishers as a group are not outstanding womanizers or (if it can be permitted) manizers, and spend an encouraging minimum of time loitering outside public lavatories. They may, of course, be light on Lust because they encounter it so often, vicariously, through the offerings of their more explicit authors. Conversely, whilst we have not yet found anecdote or evidence to establish the publishers of Mills & Boon's uniquely wholesome romances as deeply lecherous, their background of unremitting purity must surely drive them in that dangerous direction.

Horace Liveright was discovered on the office couch, *in flagrante*, with a voluptuous lady writer. 'I thought,' he explained subsequently, 'that an affair would help her writing.'

His self-sacrifice was not fully rewarded. The lady, a poetess, duly delivered a slim volume. It sold eight copies.

There is a persistent story – perhaps some reader of this collection will confirm it – that when an American paperback publisher decided to issue some classics he determined that *Oliver Twist* should be the first title, and that the jacket should catch the eye.

It did. It showed Oliver Twist as a muscular waif of indeterminate age, somewhere between eleven and twenty-one. Through a gruel-induced steam he was looking wolfishly at a female waif, also of indeterminate age although her tattered shift revealed a notable pectoral development. The caption was straightforward: '"More," he cried, "More!" He was insatiable!'

We are not gullible enough to believe the tale that the same publisher's edition of *Twelfth Night* bore the sales caption: '"Not again!" she cried!'

Sidney Hodgson, of the celebrated book auctioneers of Chancery Lane, was a kind and good man who, in the nature of his work, had sometimes to handle erotica or pornography. One day, according to O. F. Snelling, he looked fleetingly at a book of this kind – he had no enthusiasm for the *genre* – and failed to observe closely the intricate gilt designs round the fine binding. Had he looked closely he would have recognized them as minute repetitions of the male genitalia.

'Oh, how nice,' he said innocently. 'Straight-grained full gilt morocco. And richly tooled.'

Saul Bellow believed that to get a woman it was only necessary to say that he was a writer: 'It's an aphrodisiac,' he observed. William Saroyan however was more of a realist: 'Pretty women swarm around everybody but writers. Plain intelligent women *somewhat* swarm around writers.'

Alan Steele, bookseller, publisher, printer, editor for more than half of this century, was required as a young man to subscribe a daring novel, translated from the French and called *Short Pants*, to the London book trade. One of his calls was on Frank Denny, bookseller in the Strand and elsewhere. Denny received reps in a confessional-sized office where none was called upon to question his decision about anything. He perused the novel which Steele showed him. As he flicked through its pages, his countenance grew more and more stern. One particular word on which his eye alighted inflamed him.

'Young man,' he thundered, 'why are you dealing in this filth?' He ordered him from the cubicle.

The word to which he took exception was 'knickers'.

Jonathan Cape was inclined to 'improve' manuscripts, although in his later years, as Michael Howard reported in *Jonathan Cape, Publisher*, his emendations were often 'quietly overlooked':

> Occasionally Jonathan's editorial tinkering changed the sense to suit his own ideas rather than the author's. In reading the translation of Simone de Beauvoir's *The Second Sex*, he found a passage which described a man's post-coital impulse to light a cigarette. Jonathan crossed out 'cigarette' and substituted 'pipe'.

There is a famous, much-told story. In what may be considered its original form it appeared in the *New Yorker* in 1944, in a profile of the remarkable Scribner editor, Maxwell Perkins. Ernest Hemingway, explained Perkins, used in the manuscript of *The Sun Also Rises* three probably unprintable words:

> 'What are they?' Mr Scribner asked (this was the formidable Charles rather than the kindly Arthur).
> Perkins, who never uses a stronger phrase than 'My God', and that only in moments of great emotion, found that he simply couldn't say them.
> 'Write them, then,' said Mr Scribner.
> In his chicken-track hand, Perkins scrawled two of them on a memo pad and handed it to him.
> 'What's the third word? Mr Scribner asked.
> Perkins hesitated.
> 'What's the third word?' said Mr Scribner again, giving the pad back to him. Finally Perkins wrote it. Mr Scribner glanced at the pad. 'Max,' he said, shaking his white head, 'what would Hemingway think of you if he heard that you couldn't even write that word?'

Passed from mouth to mouth, however, the tale took on a life of its own, elaborated with each retelling. Here is what can best be described as the folk version.

One morning Mr Arthur Scribner was telephoned by a nervous young editor: 'Mr Arthur, this new young author – Mr Hemingway – he's used a *word*.'

Mr Arthur faced the situation. Bravely, with barely a tremor, he said, 'Tell me the word,' and wrote it down carefully on a pad, all four letters.

It was at lunchtime that his secretary, a conscientious and refined young woman who always checked his desk for instructions at that hour, was found in some distress. For there was the fateful word, under the pad's heading: 'Things I Must Do Today.'

The solicitor Michael Rubinstein acted for Penguin in the celebrated *Lady Chatterley* case in 1960. He recalls:

> When it transpired that Penguin were to be prosecuted, I interviewed many potential witnesses and eventually lined up seventy-two. These included Aldous Huxley who wired that he would, if required, fly over from the States. And T. S. Eliot who later, during the trial, sat with his wife in the cold corridor outside Court No. 1 at the Old Bailey in case the prosecution sought to rely on his harsh criticism of the book published some thirty years earlier; but in the event no mention of that was made and Tom Eliot was spared the risk of having to face aggressive cross-examination on his change of mind about D. H. Lawrence's most controversial work.
>
> One of the thirty-six witnesses selected by Gerald Gardiner, who led the team of defence counsel, was a very popular novelist. His name, it was felt, would already be well known to the jury, unlike the names of most of the others. I had arranged for him to attend at the Old Bailey in good time but when his name was called he did not come forward. The Usher was sent out to shout his name in the corridor. At least the jury would know he was on our side, so his actual evidence was of less consequence at that point in the trial. The next witness on our list was called, duly took the oath in the witness box and the trial proceeded, ultimately to Penguin's acquittal. At a party some weeks later I encountered our recalcitrant supporter. Seeing me, he looked only a little sheepish. However, he chose a suitable opportunity to sidle up to me and whisper, in tones which must have carried to nearly all corners of the room, 'Sorry I missed it. As a matter of fact I was in Wales having a good fuck.' What a lucky chap, I thought, to have picked up the four-letter jargon so quickly. For of course, he'd anticipated by a day or two the opening of the floodgates to the permissive society.

Allen Lane, as a rich successful bachelor, had every opportunity of chasing girls. Jack Morpurgo's biography, *King Penguin*, suggests that he rather enjoyed his dubious reputation:

> . . . the number of women who let it be known that they had shared a bed with him was at least one quarter as many as the number of those who, by public reputation supported by his mischievously ambiguous twinkle, were thought to have given their all for Penguin.

Morpurgo further records that Lane was 'perversely enthralled by the delights of letting each and every one suffer from the knowledge that there were others!'

> His sister Norah, fresh from a Quaker school and left to man the phone at Talbot Square, was given instructions to find out which of four girls called Phyllis was calling: Phyllis from the North, Phyllis from the South, Phyllis from the West, or Phyllis from the East?

She had been a successful novelist. She had also enjoyed a long and busy social life at a very nobby level, so the lady's (actually, Lady's) publisher looked forward to receiving her promised autobiography. It arrived: it was excellent, filled with engaging reminiscences of a glittering world. What troubled her publisher was the title: *Under Five Queens*.

The author was elderly and innocent of the latest Anglo-American usages and nuances. The publisher was infinitely proud of the letter which he finally devised and sent, suggesting that a better title might be found.

It proved only too successful. The lady replied enthusiastically: 'Your kind letter points me straight to the title that we *must* use for my reminiscences. *Memorable Balls*.'

Phyllis from the East

In the late 1960s Robert (soon to be Sir Robert) Lusty, then in command at Hutchinson, visited Japan. A Mrs Kitamoura, who worked for Hutchinson's Japanese agents, was deputed to look after him and, in Lusty's words, 'was assiduous in her attentions and conducted me with exquisite charm through the complications of shopping and the visitation of shrines she felt it necessary for me to see.'

Nevertheless, Mr Lusty's secretary was a little startled to open a letter for him, shortly after his return from Tokyo, in which Mrs Kitamoura opened: 'Dear and beloved gentleman, I hope you are still in the mood.'

AVARICE

Here two extraordinary, larger-than-life publishers, Sir Stanley Unwin (1884–1968) and Joseph Malaby Dent (1849–1926) are in danger of stealing the show.

Sir Stanley was mean, vain, rude and, in due course, rich, yet it is impossible not to admire his remorseless application and energy, his total professionalism as book publisher and as salesman of the books he published. If he said that 150 yards from the port gates in Lisbon there was an alley to the left where a small, intoxicated bookseller resided, willing to buy (and pay for) books in the English tongue, then there was. The emotions that Sir Stanley so strongly aroused even included – just here and there – affection.

One of the first British publishers to take full advantage of the advent of intercontinental air travel after the Second World War, Sir Stanley Unwin was once on his way to Australia. He arrived at Athens airport with four hours to wait before the departure of a connecting flight. Four hours in Athens: what should he do to pass the time? Most publishers would, perhaps, have visited the Parthenon. Not Sir Stanley: he went into the city and collected four overdue accounts.

He visited Iceland in 1934, and sent a telegram to the office. It read, economically: HAPPILY ARRIVED SUNSHINE. His colleague Charles Furth commented drily: 'Never thought of that as a nickname for S.U.'

No collection of anecdotes about bookmen could be complete without the story of Sir Stanley, the tram ticket and the Frankfurt Book Fair. Here it is, as related by his nephew Philip in *The Publishing Unwins*:

> On an early visit to Germany he learned that excellent system by which one can buy, on the trams, a form of season ticket which entitles one to about ten journeys at a slightly reduced price. The ticket is punched for each journey one makes. Some sixty years later I was with him at Frankfurt one morning, at a time when he could, if he had wished, have put his hands on a six-figure sum. Disdaining the bunch of publishers waiting for taxis to take them from the Frankfurter Hof Hotel to the Book Exhibition, we scooted off to the nearby tram stop.
>
> 'Don't forget,' he said, as we stepped aboard the tram, 'you can save ten per cent by getting the season ticket.' I duly saved it. The system had been familiar to me about thirty years earlier, but I had not troubled with it since – there was always the risk of losing the damn ticket. Four days later, on the Sunday morning when I was packing up to return to London on an early flight, he looked into my room. He was clad in his dressing-gown and had come, very decently I thought, to say good-bye, as he was staying on for a few days. 'By the way,' he said, 'have you got any journeys left on your tram ticket? – if so, I'll have it!'

Sir Stanley had come up the hard way, and in his early business life he was constantly short of money. In later years he was wont to say that whilst a bookseller's assistant in Kensington, he could afford only once a week the luxury of a penny cup of tea. This indigence only served to sharpen his wits and his determination. Philip Unwin once again:

> ... it was a masterpiece of youthful ingenuity and sheer guts to have contrived to travel from Leipzig to Berlin and back (about 100 miles each way), and to live in the capital for a fortnight, on a total sum of £3, at the same time cajoling *German* booksellers to place firm orders to the value of £150 for Fisher Unwin books in *English*, when they normally took their books on sale or return. It was an achievement which he delighted to recount to any willing listener in years to come.

Even as a little boy he was celebrated as quick-thinking, careful and law-abiding. His nickname at school was 'The Holy Ghost on Wheels'.

Charles Furth, on a sales trip in darkest Africa, was stricken with some fearful local malady. Through a haze of pain he saw his companion, Sir Stanley, at his bedside feeding him with a mysterious tablet. The tablet worked. 'What was it?' inquired the convalescent.

Sir Stanley was decisive: 'Half an aspirin. I wouldn't risk any more.'

Philip Unwin recalled the cheeky office boy who said to a little group of junior office staff:

'D'you know what Sir Stanley does with his old clothes?' only to rap out in reply, 'Wears them!'

'. . . the Greater Glory of God!'

Enter J. M. Dent. He, too, was both rude and mean – he considered the best advertisements to be those which contained the most words. He was ill-educated, with a doubtful grasp of the English language. Worst of all, he was a bully with a genuine relish for terrorizing subordinates who had no chance of hitting back. Yet his vision of Everyman's Library, of making the great books of the world available to humble people at prices they could afford, was as marvellous as that of Allen Lane and Penguin thirty years later. Dent was fifty-seven when he published the first Everyman title, but his dynamic energy was such that within twelve months he and his long-suffering, ill-paid assistant, Ernest Rhys, had issued no fewer than 150 books under that imprint.

J. M. Dent once had the idea of publishing an Everyman Bible, and summoned Ernest Rhys to discuss it. After a two-hour harangue from Dent, Rhys nervously asked what his reward in the matter of this Bible might be. '*Reward?*' thundered Dent. 'Your reward would lie in the Greater Glory of God!'

Dent used to get authors to write to him for nothing. He used to call it *con amore* – he thought it meant 'for love'.

These eminently successful businessmen had many predecessors with similarly ingrained concern about how their money was disposed. The following dialogue between two men lunching together to celebrate an important new agreement has a curiously modern ring:

A: 'Come on, old chap, let's have another bottle of wine.'
B: 'Very well, but how much will it cost?'
A: 'Oh, five pounds, I suppose; but you don't have to worry. This is all on me, you know.'
B: 'Well, why don't you just give me three pounds and keep two pounds for yourself? That way we shall both be richer.'

This canny story (prices adjusted for inflation) in fact comes from a Scottish literary journalist of the eighteenth century, Henry Mackintosh.

Mackintosh also records the frosty reception given in Edinburgh to Dr Johnson by a Scottish aristocrat, who listened for some time to the great man talking away at his most brilliant, then tendered him a shilling: 'About the right payment for a performing bear, I think.'

Thomas Tegg, an early nineteenth-century publisher and remainder merchant ('I was the broom that swept the booksellers' warehouses'), produced cheap reprints of old authors, careless of paper and print and accuracy of text. One day, he handed his printer the reprint order of Milton's *Paradise Lost*, and supplied the paper for the edition.

The paper ran short before all twelve Books of the masterpiece were completed.

'I cannot afford any more,' said Tegg. 'How far can you go with what you have?'

'To the end of the Tenth Book,' replied the printer.

'That will do,' said Tegg. 'When you come to the end of Book Ten, put "Finis" and print no more.'

The publishing brothers Tinsley, William and Edward, are described in *Publishing and Bookselling* by Mumby and Norrie as 'a curious pair'. The former 'liked to work in his shirtsleeves and could be wooed into accepting manuscripts by authors who took the trouble to play with his black cat on the counter'; the latter had a great enthusiasm for Thomas Hardy whose first novel he published in 1871. But two books later there was trouble:

> When [Hardy] published *A Pair of Blue Eyes* he had come to definite recognition. But the experience was bitter. Tinsley agreed to publish the book on condition that Hardy would pay £75 for the privilege of being published. And Hardy paid the money down.
>
> Tinsley then sold between three and four thousand sets of this book; three volumes to the set. Hardy's star was rising in the literary firmament. He expected a cheque of some importance to come through his letter-box any day from Tinsley. But instead of the cheque, Tinsley sent him in a bill for a further £15.
>
> Hardy said this was the greatest disappointment he ever had in his life.
>
> 'Tinsley's letter worried me a great deal,' he went on. 'I hadn't much money. I didn't want to pay that bill. And I didn't want to leave Tinsley. But I resolved that I must ... I went up to see him, and I laid fifteen sovereigns on his desk, and they were hard-gotten sovereigns. At the same time I told him that I must publish elsewhere in future ... Tinsley put the coins carefully in his pocket without a word. Then he leaned over his desk and broke into tears. He said that all his authors were leaving him!'
>
> (from *Just As It Happened*, Desmond Flower)

Sir Algernon Methuen, too, was known to be extremely thrifty. One of his richer authors, Stephen McKenna, met him one day in the street and asked him where he was going. The reply was that he was going to a particular art exhibition. Stephen McKenna said, 'You can't, it's closed.' 'Oh, good,' said Methuen, 'I've saved half-a-crown.'

The credit for having introduced the best-seller H. V. Morton to Methuen belongs to R. H. Havercroft, who, while working there as a lowly clerk, read Morton's articles on London when they first appeared in the *Daily Express* in 1925. Being a good Londoner himself, he was so far carried away by them as to seek an interview with his managing director and suggest diffidently that the articles might be published by the firm in book form. After a due interval for tut-tutting ('what ever do you know about literary matters?') the suggestion was acted on. After *The Heart of London* (1925) there were four more London books, followed by six *In Search of* books – all straightforward letterpress printings with the minimum of illustration and all extremely successful, as Havercroft, who kept the publishing ledger, knew better than anyone.

In 1935 the directors remembered Havercroft's part in this profitable ten-year venture and sent for him: 'We have been very pleased with the result of your excellent H. V. Morton suggestion, and would like as a mark of the firm's gratitude to present you with a complimentary set of the ten volumes published so far, bound in real leather and signed by us all.'

Havercroft left the next day in disgust and moved to Edward Arnold as manager. Here, and with the Epworth Press after the War, he served until his death in the 1960s. His enthusiasms were for the MCC and Methodism rather than Methuen.

Chatto & Windus originated from the business of John Camden Hotten (1832–1873 – 'that somewhat notorious tradesman' according to Swinburne), for whom Andrew Chatto was manager. Hotten was not very prosperous, and Chatto told the story of a creditor who had failed dismally to get his money. He went round to Hotten's flat, fiercely determined to get satisfaction, brushed aside the woman who opened the door and stormed into the publisher's bedroom. Only when he had finished shouting did he realize that Hotten was lying there, quite dead.

Andrew Chatto knew his authors. According to Arnold Bennett he would say to a writer, 'I'm sorry, I like your book very much indeed but I can't give you more than £25 for the copyright.' The author would say: 'Oh, but Mr Chatto, that's very little,' and he would reply, 'I have the cheque in my pocket.'

Sir Ernest Benn, financier and founder of a trade magazine empire, was, in the words of one of his employees, 'a hard, grim little man who scared me to death'. Shrewd, tough, teetotal, in an uncharacteristic move, when he decided to develop the book side of his business, he took on Victor Gollancz, Jewish, socialist, extravert and recently fired from teaching at Repton by Fisher the headmaster (later to be the Archbishop).

It would be nice to record that they got on a treat; in fact they disliked each other intensely and after six years, in 1927, Gollancz left to set up his own publishing firm. But in his subsequent aggressive career he never forgot one of Benn's *dicta*: 'You can lose money on a gold mine if you take long enough about it.'

A manuscript combining the dual American passions of success and religion reached the desk of Maxwell Perkins, Scribner's celebrated editor. He read it with mounting horror and took it to the firm's President, Charles Scribner, a true monster noted for his fierceness and his short memory. Perkins explained:

'It treats Christ as a super-salesman,' he said, 'a go-getter, a man with a talent for business. Of course, it might sell.'

C.S., with his long background of grave religious publishing, was properly shocked and agreed that it should be declined. When it appeared (under another imprint), however, C.S. sent for Perkins.

'How about this book?' he said. 'Why haven't we got it?'

'Why, we discussed that, Mr Scribner. I talked it all over with you a year ago and we decided to decline it.'

'You discussed it with me? You mean the manuscript came to us?'

Even Perkins was startled by this incredible evidence of C.S.'s power of forgetting.

'Why, certainly, Mr Scribner. Don't you remember that I told you it portrayed Christ as a salesman? And I added that it might sell.'

C.S. looked at him a long time without change of expression. Then, with only the faintest twinkle in his right eye, he leaned forward and pointed his finger at Perkins.

'But you didn't tell me, Mr Perkins, that it would sell 400,000 copies!'

(from *Of Making Many Books*, Roger Burlingame)

Mary Webb's sombre Shropshire novels were first put on the map in a big way after her death, by a eulogy of *Precious Bane* from Stanley Baldwin at a public dinner in 1928 – after which Cape acquired all her publishing rights and put out a pocket uniform edition. In Mary Webb's own lifetime the novels had sold so moderately that at her death in 1927 she left only £937. Her husband, Henry Webb, then married an art student, Kathleen Wilson, and died in his turn in 1938, leaving his widow £35,804, mainly made up of his accumulated royalties on his first wife's novels.

In 1941 Jonathan Cape married, as his third wife, the widowed Mrs Henry Webb, and thus found himself in a position, for the remaining twenty years of his life, to enjoy not merely the considerable publishing profits from the Mary Webb novels, but the author's considerable royalties as well (See Matthew xiii. 12.).

George Depotex recalls a Foyles Educational outing to the sea. Gilbert Foyle (the G. of W. & G. Foyle, the celebrated Charing Cross Road booksellers) was there; it was a splendid occasion.

> The Eastbourne brass band played for us. Gilbert was their patron, buying their uniforms and instruments, and we were given a splendid lunch.
>
> It was a sunny day, but very windy. In the afternoon I was one of a party playing on the putting green at Beachy Head. Alerted by shouting, I looked up from addressing my ball to see Gilbert Foyle's hat floating past me on the breeze towards the cliff edge. Using my putter like a sword I slashed out, knocked the hat out of the air and pinned it to the ground with my club.
>
> Gilbert came running up. I waited for words of praise and thanks. ''Ere, careful, lad,' he grumbled, 'that's me best 'at!'

Evelyn Waugh was a publisher's son, and had much to do with publishers, yet this passage from *Vile Bodies* suggests a lack of affection for the species.

Waugh's hero, Adam Fenwick-Symes, has just had the only copy of his completed manuscript seized and burnt by a customs officer. He goes to see his publishers (not the senior director, Mr Rampole, but the junior director, Sam Benfleet):

Adam explained the circumstances of the destruction of his autobiography. There was a longish pause while Sam Benfleet thought.

'What worries me is how are we going to make that sound convincing to old Rampole.'

'I should think it sounded convincing enough.'

'You don't know old Rampole. It's sometimes very difficult for me, Adam, working under him. Now if I had my own way I'd say, "Take your own time. Start again. Don't worry . . ." But there's old Rampole. He's a devil for contracts, you know, and you did say, didn't you . . .? It's all very difficult. You know, I wish it hadn't happened.'

'So do I, oddly enough,' said Adam.

'There's another difficulty. You've had an advance already, haven't you? Fifty pounds, wasn't it? Well, you know, that makes things very difficult. Old Rampole never likes big advances like that to young authors. You know I hate to say it, but I can't help feeling that the best thing would be for you to repay the advance – plus interest, of course, old Rampole would insist on that – and cancel the contract. Then if you ever thought of re-writing the book, well, of course, we should be delighted to consider it. I suppose that – well, I mean, it would be quite convenient, and all that, to repay the advance?'

'Not only inconvenient, but impossible,' said Adam in no particular manner.

There was another pause.

'Deuced awkward,' said Sam Benfleet. 'It's a shame the way the Customs House officers are allowed to take the law into their own hands. Quite ignorant men, too. Liberty of the subject, I mean, and all that. I tell you what we'll do. We'll start a correspondence about it in the *New Statesman* ... It is all so deuced awkward. But I think I can see a way out. I suppose you could get the book rewritten in time for the Spring List? Well, we'll cancel the contract and forget all about the advance. No, no, my dear fellow, don't thank me. If only I was alone here I'd be doing that kind of thing all day. Now instead we'll have a new contract. It won't be quite so good as the last, I'm afraid. Old Rampole wouldn't stand for that. I'll tell you what, we'll give you our standard first-novel contract. I've got a printed form here.

'May I just see the terms?'

'Of course, my dear fellow. They look a bit hard at first, I know, but it's our usual form. We made a very special case for you, you know. It's very simple. No royalty on the first two thousand, then a royalty of two and a half per cent, rising to five per cent on the tenth thousand. We retain serial, cinema, dramatic, American, colonial and translation rights, of course. And, of course, an option on your next twelve books on the same terms. It's a very straightforward arrangement really. Doesn't leave room for any of the disputes which embitter the relations of author and publisher. Most of our authors are working on a contract like that. ... Splendid. I understand perfectly, and I'll square old Rampole somehow, even if it comes out of my director's fees.'

Some said that Stanley Bond of Butterworths was mean. He certainly had the reputation of under-paying both his authors and his staff. Once a packing-case of books left the warehouse bearing the inscription: 'The wages of sin are death, but the wages of Butterworths are worse.'

The canny Scots manager of the Collins Bibles Division was called from Glasgow to London to be congratulated by the Chairman and the Board on his achieving an especially impressive level of sales. His head was not turned by the praise lavished upon him; rather did he reflect on the higher targets he would doubtless be set in the future. 'Oh, Sir William,' he demurred gloomily, 'ah'm only making a rod for ma own back.'

André Deutsch, shrewd observer of publishing economics, claims that the business sense of a publisher is in inverse proportion to the wattage of the bulbs in his firm's toilets. Clarence Paget of Pan, when a customer complained that all the pages of a Pan paperback fell out in the reading: 'Of course. You don't think we want the things to last for ever . . .?'

Tom Rosenthal of Heinemann is a resourceful publisher. He was flying back from an American foray; a friendly British publisher was sitting next to him. The plane was Concorde, and there was the usual constant flow of freebies. Rosenthal shovelled them all into a bag: 'For my children, you know,' he said to his neighbour. 'Perhaps you would let them have yours, too?' There was a generous agreement, more went into the bag, and the neighbour (after wondering which of the children would smoke the free cigars) changed the subject.

'I must read that book you've just published.' He named a title. 'Perhaps you could let me have a copy?'

'My dear chap,' replied Rosenthal, in comparably generous mood, 'I'll send you one. At best trade terms, of course.'

GLUTTONY

Astonishingly, Gluttony comes out as one of the thinner sins. It is true that two of the towering monsters, J. M. Dent and Sir Stanley Unwin, were notably abstemious in the matter of bodily nourishment. But it is indeed the case that no other business is so much conducted at the lunch table.

The length and frequency of publishers' lunches is legendary. Reports that in New York three-Martini lunches have now given way to one-Perrier lunches are met by the British with scepticism. Publishers lunch authors and authors' agents, book buyers and rights buyers, other publishers and, increasingly, media people. They are still lunching them when everyone else has left the restaurant and is thinking of tea, so there should be a plethora of stories in this field.

Stories there are, of course, as far as authors are concerned: tales of the alcoholic excesses of Dylan Thomas and Brendan Behan, James Thurber, Raymond Chandler and countless others are only too familiar. But publishers, despite the evidence of many a waistband and bloodshot eye, have generally contrived a discreet suppression of the sinful facts. This section therefore produces few revelations, but it does throw some light on the curious attitudes of book people to food and drink.

Sam Westkitt was a publisher's clerk in Hutchinson in the 1930s, so ill paid that he used to keep his own pigeon trap on the windowsill by his desk. Baited at the lunch hour, in no time the trap would yield a pigeon which was swiftly decapitated and – since Westkitt's lunchtime arrangements included camp stove and frying pan – plucked, fried and eaten.

Harry Batsford died in 1951, to be succeeded by his nephew who started life as Brian Cook and became Sir Brian Batsford, distinguished both as publisher and politician.

Harry Batsford was in the best tradition of eccentrics. It is reputed that he was once married, his bride leaving him shortly after lunch on the following day. Thereafter his chief interests were books and cats.

In pursuit of the latter cause, a member of the Batsford staff would buy a quantity of fishes' heads and remnants, placing the large, newspaper-wrapped parcel on his desk. In the evenings, Harry Batsford would walk the streets of Paddington, near where he lived, dispensing tit-bits to his friends, the local cats.

Nobody grudged the cats their meal in winter, but on hot summer days sometimes the fish went off rapidly, a fearful smell permeated the building, and the parcel was consigned to the Batsford boilers.

This created a really dreadful pong, which reached Batsford's superior bookshop located in the same building. Customers entering the shop would give a sniff, at which the lady in charge would say, 'Not to worry, we're only burning Mr Harry's cats' meat.'

Harry Batsford was very much the master of his firm (although he had a partner, Mr Hannaford Smith, to whom, it is believed, he had not spoken for twenty-five years) and saw no reason to be careful about his appearance. He was reputed to buy one suit annually which he wore continually for the year – steadily filling the pockets – and then threw away.

Clarence Paget, who worked with him, recalls that he had invited a distinguished foreign publisher to lunch at his club. Paget's club was pretty snobbish, and kept an eagle eye on the demeanour and behaviour of members and their guests. Batsford announced that he would join them, and Paget awaited his arrival with some trepidation.

At first all went well: Mr Batsford had spruced himself up for the occasion and was genial (not always the case). The problem arose when they started the meal with Dublin Bay prawns. Harry Batsford made heavy weather of the use of the small tridents supplied for the disembowelling of these tasty creatures. He rummaged among the extraordinary detritus in his pockets and finally produced a sturdy pair of nail scissors. With these, triumphantly, he cut the first large prawn in half, whereupon each end whistled like a rocket through the dining room and past the scandalized members.

Clarence Paget resigned from the club soon afterwards. He continues to insist, however, that there is no connection between the two events.

Some associates of Harry Batsford were anxious to persuade him into a course of action. It was undoubtedly going to be a difficult affair – it involved paying out more money – and as a softening-up preliminary he was given a large glass of a carefully selected, expensive and unusually excellent claret.

Batsford took a sip and put down his glass. He scrabbled for a while in his unique pockets. He then produced two saccharine tablets, stirred them briskly into the claret with a pencil, and drank the mixture with every appearance of relish.

Children's book editors nowadays tend to be clear-eyed and unsentimental: it wasn't always so.

One children's editor went to spend Christmas with some farmer friends. She arrived late in the evening. 'There,' said her friends, 'is our Christmas dinner,' and they pointed to two freshly plucked geese.

The farmers were out the following morning when their six-year-old daughter approached the editor. 'Where,' she demanded, 'are our two pet geese? I can't see them outside.'

The editor thought quickly.

'My dear,' she said, 'I'm afraid your geese have died. And they've gone where all good geese go – they've gone to heaven.'

'Oh,' said the child blankly, 'I thought we were going to eat them.'

Victor Gollancz, whose social conscience was as highly developed as his love of good living, once took a young author to lunch at the Savoy. He plied his guest with champagne, smoked salmon, venison . . . as the author munched away, Gollancz merely puffed at his cigar. Eventually the young man plucked up courage to ask his host:

'Aren't you having anything to eat, Mr Gollancz?'

'Good gracious, no.' Puff, puff. 'How can anyone eat today when that unfortunate prisoner is being hanged at Pentonville?'

Sir Stanley Unwin once took a guest to lunch at the Reform Club, and as they finished giving their order to the club servant, Sir Stanley turned to his companion.

'I suppose you will want a drink,' he said. 'Of course, I don't drink myself; I will just take water. But if you must have a drink, I'm told the cider here is very good.'

He was a distinguished author in his special field but not – by the standards of the Swinging Sixties – trendy. His literary agent asked him to a dinner party and, after the meal, offered him a cigarette: indeed, to his mild surprise, lit it and passed it to him.

He smoked it peacefully for a while, reflecting that the tobacco probably wasn't Virginian, when he became aware of a lull in conversation and of the other guests looking at him avidly. 'Is there,' he enquired mildly, 'anything wrong with my cigarette?'

'It's not a cigarette,' said his literary agent crossly, 'it's a joint.'

'*Aren't you having anything to eat, Mr Gollancz?*'

One of the lurking terrors of publishers is libel. They believe that ingenious complainants, simulating aggrievedness over the most innocent or accidental of comments, can instruct their lawyers to pounce, forcing withdrawal of books just as they are launched amid hopes of success and mulcting authors and publishers of disproportionately large damages and costs (it is generally the publisher and his expensive insurance policy that bears the brunt of the claims). Publishers also believe that the juries involved in such cases usually include a preponderance of lunatics. It helps publishers in such cases if the author concerned is tractable. Some authors are; others . . .

In 1962 an extract in the *Observer* from a Brendan Behan book published by Hutchinson brought a prompt complaint of libel from a Dublin lawyer. The lawyers for the newspaper and the publisher thought that a moderate and apologetic stance might achieve a modest settlement, and the author was asked to assist in their negotiations.

Brendan joined them having, as the phrase went, 'indulged his hobby'. He arrived loudly effing and blinding, progressed to singing a maudlin ditty and moved to the verge of a punch-up with his publisher's solicitor. He finally made it abundantly clear that he saw any attempt to placate the claimant as unforgiveable treachery.

Brendan was *not* a tractable author.

WRATH

The book trade is generally thought of as reasonably peaceable, and there is a grain of truth in that belief. But this section reveals a fair amount of anger, irritation and gall.

Authors not unexpectedly rail against publishers. Fairly typical of their tirades is that of John Dryden in 1706 against his publisher, Jacob Tonson:

> With leering looks, bull-faced and freckled fair;
> With two left legs, and Judas-coloured hair,
> And frowzy pores, that taint the ambient air.

It is only fair to add that Nicholas Rowe later redressed the balance:

> Thou, Jacob Tonson, were to my conceiving,
> The cheerfullest, best honest fellow living.

The charitable Rowe appears to have been in a minority. Publishers are probably now hardened to the Barabbas tag, but it is worth remembering that booksellers have also aroused writers' ire. Charles Lamb wrote of them: 'They are Turks and Tartars when they have poor authors at their beck . . . you know what a rapacious, dishonest set these booksellers are.'

Peter Pindar was even fiercer: 'Booksellers drink of their wine in the manner of the heroes in the hall of Odin – out of authors' skulls.'

Today's booksellers might, however, make the rejoinder that nearly two hundred years ago booksellers performed many of the functions of publishers and so were tarred with their vices.

Publishers, if only in sensible self-interest, do not usually become excessively angry with their authors, although we have some prize examples to the contrary here; one cannot help but feel, nonetheless, that they were sorely tried.

Most writers, like all creative artists, start out with a considerable degree, perhaps a necessary degree of egocentricity, compounded by loneliness and a need to fend for themselves. This may be a valuable preliminary asset. Subsequent success can add to these an arrogance which leads them to complain bitterly about their readers, their publishers, their reviewers and even the benefactors who give them literary awards. It is absurd to expect that gifted people are necessarily nice.

Even so, it is rare for an author to wish his publisher quite as ill as did Norman Douglas. In 1921 he declared, 'Martin Secker has sent me his account up to last June (all faked, of course, but all his accounts are faked) . . . But he knows, all right, what's coming in. Don't imagine Secker is an *ordinary* villain like John Lane, or Dent, or Fisher Unwin!!!' Douglas had earlier expressed the urgent wish that somebody would 'bugger Secker with a pineapple'.

Authors have been known to rewrite their books when they are already in proof – Thomas Carlyle was notorious for it – incurring considerable extra cost. They don't always see it from the publisher's point of view. George Bernard Shaw, exasperated when his publisher Grant Richards charged him £10 6s for 'author's alterations and extra proofs'

pertaining to *Plays Pleasant and Unpleasant* in excess of the amount allowed by custom, rendered his own account which calculated that he was, in fact, owed £281 8s 9d by his publisher:

30*th Sept.* 1898

G. BERNARD SHAW

PITFOLD

HASLEMERE,

SURREY,

in a/c with Grant Richards

	£	s.	d.
Minimum customary allowance to Author for proof *correction*			
Pleasant Plays	10	0	0
Unpleasant Plays..	10	0	0

Services rendered as Typographical Expert by Author
to publisher

	£	s.	d.		£	s.	d.
Choice of type	5	5	0				
Design of page, margins, etc..................	2	2	0				
Choice of paper	2	2	0				
Design of title page	10	10	0				
Inspection of proofs..............................	52	10	0				
Choice of binding	2	2	0				
Consultations with publisher.................	105	0	0				
Letters of Instruction	63	0	0				
Personal instruction (no charge)	—						
					242	11	0
Extra proof corrections in style of typesetting in the interest of the Publisher's reputation					21	0	0
					283	11	0
Less amount charged in Publisher's a/c for 'Author's alterations and extra proofs'.....................					10	6	0
					273	5	0
Interest at 6% for 6 months.................................					8	3	9
					£281	8	9

(from Grant Richards, *Author Hunting*)

Publishers and authors alike have suffered at the hands of printers.

In Psalm cxix. 166 – 'Princes have persecuted me without a cause' – the word 'princes' was set as 'printers' in an early edition of the Authorized Version, which quickly became known as the Printers' Bible.

And the unfortunate author Edmund Gosse suffered fearfully when he completed an essay on Robert Browning with the sentence 'On December 12th Browning died, faint but pursuing.' When it reached him in galley proof, he found the whole proof so thick with niggling and pedantic printer's queries that, after dealing carefully with each one, Gosse could not help relieving his feelings of frustration by scrawling in huge, widely separated capitals across the bottom corner of the galley the one word R A T S !

The printer had the last word. The sentence appeared as 'On December 12th Browning died, faint but pursuing rats.'

In 1929, a 'sensational incident' occurred at the sixth annual guest night dinner of the Book Publishers' Representatives Association. Edgar Wallace, his thrillers then at the height of their huge success, addressed the throng. A veteran traveller rose to his feet ...

H. E. Alden's remarks, perhaps clumsily phrased, were no doubt intended to be humorous, but Edgar did not see it like that. H. E. Alden said that he had never read one of Edgar Wallace's books; he had spoken to his friend on the right and he had never read one, and the same with his friend on the left. But if Edgar Wallace would send him an autographed copy of one, he would be delighted to begin. Here Edgar Wallace, with the crispness of one of his own pistol shots, interpolated: 'Can you read?'

(from *Representative Majority*, Arthur Thrush)

Sydney Cockerell, head of the Fitzwilliam Museum at Cambridge for nearly thirty years from 1908, was a calculating literary entrepreneur of enormous energy and ingenuity. Initiating and maintaining correspondence with persons of literary distinction so that after their death he could sell their letters was a practice to which he admitted without shame. He took early to his bed in Kew, entertained his many visitors daily to tea and carried on his multifarious concerns without ever getting up for some ten years before he actually died.

T. E. Lawrence was one of the few who ever got the better of him. Hearing that Cockerell, as Hardy's literary executor, had refused Mrs Hardy permission to quote something in an anthology in which she was interested, Lawrence stormed off to Cambridge on his Brough motorcycle and threatened to remove from the walls of the Fitzwilliam the original of the famous portrait of himself by Eric Kennington which he had given to the Museum. Cockerell refused to give way, so Lawrence removed the portrait with his own hands and took it home to Bovington Camp on his motorcycle, intending to give it to the Ashmolean in Oxford instead. It is in fact now there, but Lawrence was killed in his final motorcycle accident before he could arrange to take it there in person.

George Robertson, the enduring half of Angus & Robertson, was an increasingly influential bookseller and publisher in Australia from 1886 until his death in 1933. He had a blunt way with would-be authors. He returned a novel to the Honourable Randolph Bedford, a member of the Legislative Assembly, no less, saying: 'Your novel as a whole gives me the hump. I have opened it this minute at random (pp 63 and 94) and I ask you, "Who wants to read such tosh?"'

With a less eminently placed author he was equally brisk: 'Your stories are quite hopeless and we feel sure that you will never do anything worthwhile. Give it up and take to gardening or something that's useful in your spare time.'

But if George Robertson could write sharp letters, he was sometimes on the receiving end, too. E. J. Brady, known for his sea ballads, wrote calling him:

> the Meanest Thing I have struck in 25 years' experience of unctuous Colonial Meanness . . . the book you endeavoured to sneak from me for £20 has already brought me over £500! [This was in 1911, when money bought more.] Robbers! No, you haven't the courage of an animal. Ye are merely oily, hypocritical sneak thieves dogging with the cringing gait of Noah Claypole the steps of the unprotected infant – Australian Literature.

Gerald Duckworth was indolent. He set up his publishing firm in Covent Garden in the 1890s, and in the decade before the First World War gave himself an easy working day. He drove up from Streatham (a porter took care of the horse), drafted a few letters, strolled to the Garrick Club for lunch and bridge, signed his letters and drove home early. He saw some service in the War, as did his manager, but when Duckworth was away the manager was released to run the firm, which he did very shrewdly. In 1919 he asked, reasonably enough, to be made a director of the firm to which he had given invaluable service for many years.

'No,' said Duckworth thoughtfully, 'I'm afraid not. You see, you're not quite a Gentleman.'

The manager was very angry. So angry indeed that he soon went off and started a rival firm. His name was Jonathan Cape – and his company quickly surpassed that of the gentlemanly Gerald Duckworth.

Joseph Malaby Dent was known behind his back as 'Limping Sin' and was the kind of publisher, as we have seen, that Frank Swinnerton might describe as a ruffian. Dent was an uneducated man: his malapropisms were famous and he once thundered at his senior traveller that he 'mustn't let the ground grow under his feet'.

He was also of uncertain temper and, according to Swinnerton, a hectoring bully of the worst kind. When he set off for two or three weeks' holiday in Italy there was indescribable relief at Aldine House: everyone from fellow directors to office boy rejoiced as he departed and immense cheerfulness broke out. There was one dreadful occasion when he missed his train at Victoria Station, and returned untimely to this scene of distressing happiness . . .

Jonathan Cape held that the only proper basis for a publishing decision was a completed manuscript and harboured a strong resentment of authors who, after receiving an advance, failed to deliver. Hugh Kingsmill was commissioned in 1936 to write his autobiography but died in 1949 without having produced it. Michael Howard recorded in *Jonathan Cape, Publisher*:

> When Michael Holroyd began to write his biography of Kingsmill, he called twice on Cape while gathering material. On one of these occasions Jonathan produced the contract for the autobiography as evidence that Hugh was unreliable (which indeed he was), having taken money for work he did not do.
> 'But,' Holroyd exclaimed, 'he died!'
> 'And whose fault was that?' demanded Jonathan.

An anecdote of aggressive salesmanship for the august house of Scribners involves a textbook salesman in the West, when parts of that region were still in the grip of Calvinism. A member of an adoption board had been persuaded by the Scribners man to vote for the purchase of a series of primary books, the *Springfield Readers*, but later he had qualms. Just before the adoption vote was due, this man went to the publisher's agent and, with a haggard voice, said:

> 'I have spent the night on my knees praying for guidance, and after my long vigil I know that God will not let me vote for the *Springfield Readers*.'
> The agent turned to him with clenched fists.
> 'You vote for those readers anyway,' he shouted, 'and then spend tonight on your knees asking God to forgive you.'

(from *Of Making Many Books*, Roger Burlingame)

Sir Robert Lusty recalls vividly his first meeting with Walter Hutchinson, that 'rogue elephant of a publisher'. He was accorded the singular favour of being given a job in the advertising department of Hutchinson without paying a premium. He was paid no wages either, and at one time found himself unpaid tutor in charge of the pupil department of five apprentices, each of whom had paid a premium to be trained. His first meeting with his new boss was a dramatic one. Hutchinson was wont to summon his terrified staff to his presence by means of a system of buzzers and flashing lights, and some three weeks after Lusty had joined the firm a light summoned him, too.

Lusty entered. Mrs Webb, Hutchinson's secretary, sat in the window overlooking Simpkin Marshall in Paternoster Lane, whilst he stood behind an enormous desk covered with the impedimenta of his multifarious companies – eventually there were to be 165 of them. He had the design for a wrapper in his hand, for Walter Hutchinson passed everything – all the advertisements, all the wrappers. This one was for some romantic novel with an attractive girl of the 1920s on the front.

'This is no bloody good, Lusty. You are Lusty?'

'Yes, I am.'

'This is no bloody good!' And he slashed a pencil right through the finished drawing. 'If I'm going to pay four guineas for a jacket I want more paint than this.' He looked at his new member of staff.

'You're Lusty?'

'Yes.'

'Well, I can tell you this, Lusty. Nothing's gone right since you've been here. And you're ruining the firm.'

It was a charming thought that after three weeks this beginner had succeeded in bringing the great empire of Hutchinson to its knees. Mrs Webb led Lusty to the door saying 'Never mind,' as though she was his nurse.

The charge, 'You're ruining the firm!' was always Walter Hutchinson's last line of attack. Desmond Elliott (who, at the tender age of nineteen, was made advertising manager of the vast Hutchinson empire only to discover a few weeks later that he was the only person to apply for the job) recalls that regularly on a Monday morning, Mr Walter would ring. 'It's no use, Elliott, you've got to go. Yesterday, alone, you cost me £15,000.' This happened so often that Elliott began to keep a tally. By the time Walter Hutchinson died, Elliott had lost him over three quarters of a million pounds.

Every Friday when Walter Hutchinson was in residence at his country seat (he flew a flag to indicate his presence) proofs of the huge advertisements that Hutchinson took in *The Sunday Times* and the *Observer* were put on a train for him to see.

Of course, the publishing house was open for business until 1 o'clock on Saturdays and corrections could be given to newspapers until noon in those far-off and hard-working days.

One Saturday at about five minutes to one, Mr Walter rang Desmond Elliott, the advertising manager, very crossly. 'Elliott,' he barked, 'it's no use. You've got to go and this advertisement will all have to be changed!'

'But, Mr Walter, they're *printing*.'

A pause and then a roar . . .

'Well, STOP them!'

'You're ruining the firm!'

When he died in 1971, John Baker was mourned as a remarkable and innovative publisher, and he frequently told this story of his earliest publishing days.

His first job in the mid 1920s was as a junior Macmillan editor. When the Macmillan packers went on strike (they were trying, unsuccessfully, to resist a wage reduction of 10/- a week down to £3) Baker – who came from a family of compositors – showed where his sympathies lay by joining the packers' picket line.

When the strike was failed and over, Macmillan intimated their anger at his action. Harold Macmillan – now made the Earl of Stockton – sent for him and told him that, to enable him to fulfil his sympathies, he would not in future work for the firm as an editor – but as a packer.

John Menzies is a large, well-established and hard-headed chain of Edinburgh-based booksellers. Sometime around 1930 their buyer was a Mr Mackenzie, a notable tough nut – and short-tempered, too.

Harry Clifford, representing the publisher Edward Arnold, visited Menzies one day, hardly recovered from an attack of influenza. He was told by one of the clerks that by coincidence old Mackenzie had just returned to work after a similar affliction. Clifford decided to put his customer in a good temper.

'I'm sorry to hear of your illness, Mr Mackenzie,' he began. 'What was the matter with you?'

Abruptly: 'Just influenza.'

'How did it take you, Mr Mackenzie? The after effects can be very bad.'

'In me legs.'

'How strange, Mr Mackenzie. It affects me in the head.'

Mackenzie looked up crossly: 'Aye, aye, Mr Clifford, it aye affects ye in the weakest pairts.'

Jokes in the bookselling business are pretty dangerous. Ian Norrie, the owner of the High Hill Bookshop in Hampstead, in a moment of irritation when the patter of tiny feet in his shop had become markedly clamorous instructed a colleague, 'Please write out a notice stating CHILDREN OF PROGRESSIVE PARENTS ADMITTED ONLY ON LEADS, and stick it on the door.'

The book world heard about it. The *Daily Mirror* reproduced the notice, which although legible was not exactly a calligraphic masterpiece, and commented pungently on the dire behaviour of the young and their mums in shops. Other papers also carried the story, which was quoted on radio and got into David Piper's *Companion Guide to London*.

On the whole it provoked amusement, but not from one lady who wrote to the local paper, the *Ham and High*, to complain of the implicit indignity conveyed by the notice, which in a fine, misplaced rage she declared as reading: PARENTS OF PROGRESSIVE CHILDREN ADMITTED ONLY ON LEADS.

Every author thinks he is his publisher's *only* author, and expects instant decisions on manuscripts submitted. It sometimes takes longer than that to reach a conclusion.

One impatient author sent his book, unsolicited, to Michael Joseph, in the days when Michael himself was in charge. The author impatiently initiated a series of telegrams demanding news. After four or five had produced no response, he tried the 'other interest' tactic: MUST HAVE DECISION ON MANUSCRIPT AS OTHER IRONS IN FIRE. M.J., tried beyond his limited endurance, terminated the correspondence: SUGGEST REMOVING IRONS AND INSERTING MANUSCRIPT.

PRIDE

Sir Stanley Unwin, inescapably, comes up again here. So do Sir Allen Lane (1902–1970) and Walter Hutchinson (1888–1950).

Allen Lane got into publishing through his uncle, John Lane. He was certainly not literary. (Charles Clark met him in 1960: 'I wanted to sparkle about Zola: he talked about apples.') But the marvellous concept of Penguin Books – they were launched in 1935 – quickly made him a successful and rich young publisher. He was shrewd, unlikeable, a womanizer (as we have seen), liked to see his staff quarrelling creatively and hired and fired with small compunction.

His firings were as nothing, however, compared with Walter Hutchinson's. He succeeded to a family firm and carried it on with an expansionist programme reminiscent of the South Sea Bubble. Fortunately his eccentric callousness in innumerable and unreasonable sackings was matched by considerable absentmindedness, so that not all the dismissals stuck. A notorious bully, his explosions had a certain splendour:

'May I have another half-crown a week, Mr Walter?'

'Don't be a bloody fool. It costs me three pounds a week to keep one of my horses.'

Hutchinson didn't enjoy his wealth – it was said that he got real pleasure only from playing the horses (he was very bad at it) and playing ping-pong with the children's nanny (he was better at that). He always hoped – vainly – for a knighthood.

He inevitably had some bestsellers, despite his reiterated warning to his editors, 'Never talk to authors.' But the following story by Jim Reynolds, then just beginning a long British publishing career, shows how unwitting was at least one of his big successes:

> A young man called Raymond, not very gainfully employed in the showrooms of the book wholesalers Simpkin Marshall, a few doors away, had been whiling away the hours reading American thrillers and had understandably decided that anything the Americans could do, he could do better. He wrote a story and gave it to a writer friend of mine who brought it to me. I read it and immediately recognized that I had in my hand a bestseller that Mr Walter would never allow us to publish. The rule was that 'at least two favourable reports' must be sent to the chairman if we wanted his approval, and I knew that our regular readers wouldn't see it my way. The obvious solution was forgery, so I sat down and wrote a couple of excellent reports under assumed names and in due course we were permitted to pay Mr Raymond a £30 advance for a novel called *No Orchids for Miss Blandish* which was published under the pseudonym James Hadley Chase.

Incidentally, Desmond Elliott avers that a French publisher later pirated the book under the title *Pas de begonias pour Madame Dugommier.*

Like some other notable publishers Hutchinson was in no way literary and when he died, rich and unhappy and by his own hand, Edmond Segrave, the Jesuit-trained editor of *The Bookseller*, did not actually call him a ruffian but was not overly Christian in the obituary he wrote. It concluded as follows:

> To [Hutchinson's] secretiveness was allied an uninhibited capacity for self-glorification . . . Some members of the book trade were irritated by this sort of thing, but the majority found it too ridiculous to bother about. To many of his fellow publishers he was a figure of fun; contentedly they added new items to their repertoire of Hutchinson anecdotes. But those who worked for him found little to laugh at in his eccentricities. Livelihoods could be swept away, and not infrequently were, for no other apparent cause than that 'Mr Walter' had indulged one of his unpredictable rages. It is this side of his character that will provide the least attractive chapter when the full story of Walter Hutchinson is told.

Segrave was proof against Walter Hutchinson's bragging and had refused to carry advertisements in *The Bookseller* for 'Britain's largest publisher'. This led to a court case. Hutchinson was awarded damages – of £2. Subsequently, when Mr Walter paid at auction the highest price ever for a prize bull, the facts were duly reported in the book trade's organ under the sour headline: 'Britain's biggest publisher buys Britain's costliest cow'.

Hutchinson's penchant for grandiose programmes would have led to bankruptcy had not the Second World War suddenly given immense value to huge accumulated stocks of previously unsaleable books. Sir Basil Blackwell commented wryly:

> At the beginning of the late lamented War Walter Hutchinson and Stanley Unwin had considerable stocks and they had both insured them before the War started. Unwin prudently wrote them down to the bare bone; Hutchinson wrote them up as high as he could to puff up his balance sheets. The obliging Hun came and blew both stocks to billy-ho. Unwin lost a fortune and Hutchinson made one.

Here is a Walter Hutchinson story which presents him in characteristically manic form; he was only consistent in his unpredictability.

Coming one morning into Hutchinson (née Derby) House – the only publisher's offices to contain a ballroom, a winter garden and a drawing room with an Angelica Kauffmann ceiling – Mr Walter travelled amiably up in the lift to the top floor and entered the first office on the left.

'You're awfully crowded in here,' he observed, and five heads lifted hopefully. Even more benignly he continued: 'Well, we must do something about that, mustn't we? Now, you, you and you. You're fired.'

Walter Hutchinson's celebrated arbitrariness in firing was matched by that of his contemporary, A. D. Peters, the literary agent. He sacked Peter Jansen-Smith and Clarence Paget (both later flourished in publishing) giving the same reason to each. 'I don't,' he said, 'like your face.'

There can be no greater contrast between the popular images of Walter Hutchinson and Sir Stanley Unwin.

Publishers have their own national associations, with their own gatherings and jamborees; superimposed upon them is the International Publishers Association which has jamborees the world over, in Vienna, Washington, Stockholm, Tokyo, Paris and – one year – in Florence. From there this international assemblage took the train to Rome to be blessed by the Pope.

There were a great many publishers, with Sir Stanley Unwin inevitably in the van, and even more people from other occupations awaiting the papal blessing. When it was over, one of the British publishers enquired of Sir Stanley, 'Did you have a nice little talk with the Pope?' 'No, no, I didn't,' he replied benignly. 'I pushed one or two of the others forward. You see, he knows me.'

Sir Stanley Unwin, pleasantly to Peter Schwed after three sets of tennis at the Hampstead house (but in no mood to offer hospitality): 'Thank you. I enjoyed that. The tube station is just down the road. Turn left at the third lamp-post.'

When Lady Unwin, who was the same age as Sir Stanley, asked that their massive pianola, unmoved and virtually unused for over thirty years, be jettisoned he was shocked. 'No. I shall need to play it in the evenings after you've gone.' He pre-deceased her by three years.

Ralph Vernon-Hunt, until recently head of Pan paperbacks, contributes this anecdote, so revealing of Sir Stanley's character, hitherto untold:

> One day in the early 1960s I was privileged to sit next to Sir Stanley on the plane to the Frankfurt Book Fair. Towards the end of the journey, during which I had learned much from the great man, I suggested that he should come with me into the city in the car which awaited me.
>
> 'No,' said Sir Stanley, 'I *always* take the bus, but thank you indeed.'
>
> I considered my tactics.
>
> 'Sir Stanley,' I said, determined to win, 'I understand that very sensibly you are careful with your expenditure, so I am sure that you will appreciate that riding in our car will cost you nothing and additionally will be quicker and more comfortable.'
>
> 'No,' said Sir Stanley, 'I have told you, I *always* take the bus.'
>
> Not wishing to believe that my company was so appalling, or that Sir Stanley was suffering from a rare case of bus fetishism, I decided to take the bull by the horns.
>
> 'Sir Stanley, with much respect may I suggest that you are both misguided and extremely obstinate.'
>
> There was a long silence. The plane was landing and I had been extremely impolite to one of the great men of British publishing. I trembled. Just before touchdown he gently tapped my arm and said, 'Hunt. You are an impertinent young man,' (I was over forty at the time) 'but I don't doubt your kindly intent and have now decided to accept your offer, but on two conditions. Firstly, that you drop me at the airport bus station in the city and *not* at my hotel, and secondly that you never tell anybody that I *didn't* take the bus.'
>
> I complied with the first request and, until now, have never divulged the awful secret of his car ride.

'Left at the third lamppost.'

When Philip Unwin, sincerely grieved at Walter Harrap's death, wrote a felicitous letter from the offices of Allen & Unwin it reached Harrap's offices with a neat endorsement in another hand: 'I concur with the above sentiments. S.U.'

Sir Stanley's ship berthed in Wellington. First down the gangplank, he seized the arm of his New Zealand agent waiting on the quayside and said, 'Right. Where first?'

'I thought, Sir Stanley, Harry South. He's the doyen of the Wellington booksellers.'

'I've got an entry for him.'

Sir Stanley took out his notebook, fingered the pages and read out the entry.

'South, Harry. Pompous old bore.'

On one of Allen Lane's Australian visits he stayed with the manager of the local Penguin company and toured with his deputy. Both men went to the airport to see their employer off. He shook hands pleasantly, said to the manager, 'You're out,' to the deputy, 'You're in,' and to both, 'I'm off.'

As he boarded the plane, Lane turned to his British right-hand man, Ron Blass, and said: 'May have made a mistake there: must go back and put it right.'

It was too late to do it then, but Ron Blass was sent back from London a week later with new instructions. He fired *both* men.

Allen Lane could be entirely obsessed by business, or by the prospect of new and wider business dealings. Three months after the launching of Penguin, according to his biographer, Jack Morpurgo:

> One evening in October 1935 he took Ethel Mannin to dinner. The lobster was about to be served when Miss Mannin mentioned that her American publisher was in London and leaving next day for the Continent. Without apology or explanation Allen rose from the table and went to the telephone. He did not return to the lobster or to Miss Mannin.

Sir Ernest Hodder-Williams was noted for his brevity. Writing around 1920 to Sir James Barrie, his most celebrated author whose new manuscript had not arrived a few days after its contracted delivery date:

> My dear Barrie,
> Greetings to you, and where is the script?

A few years later a bookseller ventured to complain; this was the riposte:

> Sir,
> If we cannot do business together happily, I propose that we no longer do business together at all. My traveller will call for the stock.

The bookseller arrived rapidly at Hodder & Stoughton to plead for mercy.

Jeremiah Kaplan, the enormously energetic founder of the Free Press of Glencoe, became an executive of Macmillan in America and was sent to London to manage its acquisition, Cassell, the publisher of Winston Churchill and a leading British house. Kaplan's salary was of American rather than British dimensions, and the spectacular sum was reported in *Private Eye* at precisely the wrong moment, when Cassell was in the middle of wage negotiations with the National Union of Journalists.

An employee snipped the paragraph out of the paper and pinned it to the company notice board. One of Kaplan's managers saw it, detached it and hurtled up to his boss's office.

'This was on the notice board, Jerry,' he panted, 'so I took it off right away.'

'You ass-hole,' Jerry replied, 'you should have left it there and written on it "... and worth every penny".'

Sir Arthur Norrington – of Trinity, OUP and the Clarendon Press – could be grand if he wished. When asked if his publishing business had ever rejected a bestseller he replied: 'Yes, indeed. *Decline & Fall*. Not Evelyn Waugh's; Gibbon's.'

In the 1950s, there were two kings of London's underworld, Billy Hill and Jack Spot. Heinemann published Billy Hill's recollections; Jim Reynolds, then managing director of Muller, recalls the subsequent arrival of Jack Spot and a friend at his publishing offices.

It turned out that Spot's 'friend' was his brother, who was also his mouthpiece. After offering insincere greetings I asked them what I could do for them. The ensuing conversation went something like this.

Spot	'Me brother do the talking.'
Me	'Ah.'
Brother	'Jack wants ter write 'is book.'
Me	'Memoirs I suppose?'
Brother	'Yus. 'E wants yer ter publish 'is memories.'
Me	'Well, really, I don't think. . . .'

Brother, menacingly 'Why not?'

Me, nervously 'Well, you see, Mr Spot has had some articles in the *Sunday Pictorial* and I think that . . . er . . . probably about . . . er . . . wraps it up, so to speak.'

Spot	'Balls.'
Brother	'Billy 'Ill done 'is.'
Me	'Ah yes, but Heinemann didn't do too well with it, I believe.'
Brother	'Lidy Docker come to the party an' all.'
Me	'Ah, so true. Such a *colourful* personality, don't you think . . .?'
Spot	'Balls.'
Brother	'Jack's the King. Billy don't amount ter nothin'.'

Me, evasively 'Well perhaps . . . er . . . you'd like to let me see a . . . er . . . synopsis of the proposed book – what it will . . . um . . . contain and so forth . . .?'

Brother 'Don't know nothin' abaht that. If yer give us a writer, Jack and me'll tell 'im wot ter put.'

Me, insanely 'Let me think about it. I'll call you. Would you care to leave your address and phone number?'

Spot 'That's a larf!'

Me, inspiredly 'Or perhaps you'd like to try Heinemann?'

Brother 'Yus, I guess yer right. Come on Jack – let's go see a *real* publisher!'

When, for the first time, the Macmillan Inc. top brass visited Cassell at the sign of the Belle Sauvage in Red Lion Square, Desmond Flower, Cassell's Chairman, expatiated on his company's splendid list, from the religious works of the nineteenth century to the books of Robert Graves, Nicholas Monsarrat and Winston Churchill.

'Jesus H. Christ,' interrupted one of the brass crisply, 'don't give me that prestige crap.'

Desmond Flower received a letter from an admirer of an early Nicholas Monsarrat novel (this was before the enormous success of *The Cruel Sea*), complaining that the publisher seemed to have given inadequate backing to so excellent a book. It was a meek enough complaint, which opened, 'I fear you may think this letter impertinent . . .'

Flower's answer was succinct: 'You say we may find your letter impertinent. We do. Yours faithfully.'

Barley Allison of Secker & Warburg remembers Jonathan Cape being characteristically dogmatic:

'Books on Marie Antoinette sell. Books on South America don't sell.'

'What about other books?'

'There are no other books.'

Victor Gollancz was the uncle of Michael Rubinstein, the solicitor. Rubinstein recalls that when V.G. needed legal advice after the Second World War, he and his father would call at Gollancz's shabby offices, squeezed between Henrietta Street and Maiden Lane:

> V.G. would stride restlessly round the small room from the mantelpiece where his pipe-smoking equipment lay to his cheap wooden armchair behind a desk covered with manuscripts. On the walls were paintings by his wife – a self-portrait and portraits of their five daughters – and scribbled sketches and in-jokes. From time to time minions – they might have been packers or co-directors – knocked on the door from the corridor in plain trepidation, leaving shortly, either glowing from unwonted praise or balled out, probably quite unjustly. From another door Sheila Hodges, his long-suffering right hand, emerged not infrequently to take down a dictated note standing in the doorway, or to deliver a cryptic message.
>
> On one such occasion V.G. was recounting his lunchtime visit to the tailors, Moss Bros, just around the corner. He had ordered a shirt to be delivered to Henrietta Street with the account. Sheila put her head round the door to say, 'There's someone from Moss Bros on the 'phone who says he needs three references before your shirt can be delivered.' V.G. exploded, but despite his rage did not forget the advantage of being a distinguished left-wing publisher with a Socialist government in power: 'Tell him – the Prime Minister, the Chancellor of the Exchequer and the Archbishop of Canterbury!'
>
> Moss Bros did not after all require any references.

David Kossoff, actor and religious writer, tells an affection-
ate tale about Ian Chapman, the Chairman of Collins. This
is how Kossoff became a Collins author:

> I was courted by them all and I had pretty well made up
> my mind to join Hamlyn who do a *very* hard sell. I was
> then offered dinner – not lunch, itself unusual – by
> Collins and I was given a jolly good dinner locally,
> *locally*, which I enjoyed very much and I met Ian for
> the first time. I said, 'I feel it's only right to tell you that
> I've pretty well made up my mind to join Hamlyn,'
> which he rode beautifully, and he replied, 'Oh, yes.
> They're a marvellous firm, marvellous.'
> 'They're such good merchandizers . . .'
> 'Oh, yes. Yes.'
> He was riding every punch superbly!
> 'Oh, yes,' he said, 'they've taught us all. They've
> woken up the industry. They've taught us so much
> about selling – a superb firm – and, of course, I know
> Paul Hamlyn very well and it's a remarkable organiza-
> tion. Mind you,' he continued, 'the *Establishment*
> doesn't really approve of them . . .'
> . . . and I, very new to the business said, 'Really.
> Who's the *Establishment*?'
> And he, with the sort of pause that I'm famous
> for . . .
> 'Well,' he said, 'us, I suppose!'
> I must be the only man who signed his contract there
> and then on the back of a menu!

Max Reinhardt, proprietor of The Bodley Head, went together with a number of other publishers to lunch with Lord Kemsley, the newspaper magnate. There was a reason for the generosity. When coffee had been served Kemsley addressed his guests: 'I wonder why none of you publishers have ever taken a full page in *The Sunday Times?*' At the end of the lunch, one or two of the publishers were ill-advised enough to linger behind.

Reinhardt returned to his office, called for his publicity manager, young Desmond Elliott, and informed him that The Bodley Head would be taking a full page in *The Sunday Times*, at a cost of around £2,500 – a considerable sum in publishing terms then.

'But, Mr Reinhardt, our total advertising budget for the year is £3,000.'

'That may be, Desmond, but a page in *The Sunday Times* will make me one of London's leading publishers over-night.'

There was a pause. Said Desmond, firmly: 'I don't think even two full pages in *The Sunday Times* will do that.'

Max replied sadly, 'Then I think we'll call it a day.'

'But it's only a quarter to five.'

'No, I mean you're fired.'

The President of a large American paperback house, invited to lunch on a Sunday at the Connaught Hotel in London by Desmond Elliott, appeared in an elegant turtle-necked sweater. Refused entry, even to the bar, the American disappeared to change at the hotel nearby where he was staying. One of the Connaught management apologized with exquisite delicacy to Mr Elliott.

'Where is the gentleman staying, sir?' he enquired.

'Claridges.'

'Really, sir? And they let him out like *that?*'

Michael Korda recalls an event in his early days at Simon & Schuster. He and fellow junior editor, Bob Gottlieb, were travelling down in the elevator at the end of the day; their clothes were crumpled, their shirt collars open, they clutched untidy manuscripts under their arms. Descending with them was the head of Simon & Schuster, Richard Snyder, suave and elegant in a beautifully tailored suit, Gucci shoes and with a wafer-thin black-leather document case. He looked at his minions distastefully for a moment, then observed: 'You editors. Me publisher.'

When Harold Macmillan was away from publishing as British Prime Minister and indeed a world figure, his elder brother Daniel ran the family firm of Macmillan, very authoritatively if not very well.

In the mid 1960s, after Harold Macmillan's return to the firm, a manager was discussing a project with Daniel Macmillan. 'This is a sound idea. I was talking about it to Mr Macmillan the other day. . .' His voice trailed away as he caught his chairman's eye of stone.

'I assume,' said Daniel Macmillan icily, 'that you were to talking to Mr Harold. *I* am Mr Macmillan.'

It was a literary dinner party. At the end, Anthea Lahr pointed to the film director and author Karel Reisz and said to her little son, 'That is a good writer – a very good writer indeed.' Impressed, the small boy asked: 'Can he do a "w"?'

A. S. Frere of Heinemann received the proofs of a book that contained a good deal of quotations in French. To his surprise the passages in French in the proofs were totally devoid of accents. He telephoned the production director B.F. (some said he was well-named) Oliver, who was commonly called 'O'.

'I say, O, this set of proofs I have here . . . there are no accents.'

'That's right.'

'But why?'

'I had them removed. In the first place, accents are expensive. Secondly, they spoil the look of the page. And thirdly, they are an affectation.'

SLOTH

Authors, many of them still awaiting a decision on some manuscript into which they have poured their all, may suspect that this should be a crowded section. And indeed it catches some unexpected figures, from the successful Lord Thomson to the urbane Lord Weidenfeld.

Oscar Wilde once worked as an editor for Cassell. He was taken on to run *The Ladies' World*, but the brilliant literary and social success he predicted for it did not materialize. He became bored. Much later Rider Haggard told Newman Flower (who ran Cassell for forty years from 1927) of this editorial venture:

> I remember one morning Wilde complained bitterly that he had put in a weekend of back-breaking work for Cassell. The firm was killing him. He could not sleep for worry. He appeared to be very languid and tired. I asked what had driven him to this point of exhaustion.
>
> 'Well,' explained Wilde in his slow manner, 'I spent Saturday taking a comma out of something I had written. And I had to spend Sunday putting it in again.'

In 1896, the copyright on *Who's Who*, first published in 1849, rested in the hands of Simpkin, Marshall, Hamilton, Kent & Co. and this body of men decided – surprisingly – to put it up for sale in Hodgson's auction rooms. Adam Black of A. & C. Black was interested; so was his friend George Whitaker, who had by then been publishing his famous Almanack for nearly thirty years.

The two men met at the auction rooms, decided not to bid against each other and tossed for it. Whitaker lost. Since then the profits from *Who's Who* have totalled many millions of pounds: Adam Black secured the contract for £30.

Gerald Duckworth, after publishing John Galsworthy's first two books of stories under the pseudonym John Sinjohn, was confronted in the early 1900s by the author bearing the script of *The Forsyte Saga*. In fact it was only the first novel of the saga, now known as *The Man of Property*, but Galsworthy made it clear that he was proposing a very long work indeed. According to several of those who served under him, Gerald Duckworth laboured under what might be thought a crippling disability for a publisher: a deep dislike for books as such. He was, however, a keen theatre-goer, so within a minute had given Galsworthy the advice which shaped the latter's publishing pattern for the rest of his life. 'Take your long novel,' Duckworth said, 'down the street to my friend William Heinemann who specializes in fiction, and sit down and write a play for me – I think you'd do that well.' *The Silver Box* (Duckworth, 1904) was the result, and Duckworth did all the rest of Galsworthy's dramatic output, twenty-seven plays in all, ending in 1928 with *The Roof*. But Duckworth's distaste for novels denied his firm the success, ultimately enormous, of *The Forsyte Saga*.

During the Second World War Methuen, its staff depleted by military exigencies, received a copy from America of a thriller by Jonathan Latimer, an author whom they had published several times before. *Naboth's Vineyard* was promptly despatched to the printer without a prior reading and duly published. It appears that the subsequent legal process which culminated in the book being burned by the public hangman came as a total surprise to the Methuen staff. As did the subject of the book: necrophilia. It is said (for it seems now impossible to check) that the novel contained the immortal line: 'Gee! Only one woman a year, and that a dead 'un.'

When Allen Lane was putting together the first Penguin list, his reception was hardly warm:

> Allen had not been surprised by the antipathy of most of his fellow-publishers but he had assumed that Gollancz would not go with the mob. If only as a salute from one rebel to another, Gollancz would make some cooperative gesture. Instead, when the acknowledged nobility of the trade replied to Allen's request for paperback rights with polite if glacial rejections, Gollancz merely ignored his letters. At last and in desperation Allen sent off a self-addressed and stamped postcard. On it he had typed the simple questionnaire:
>
> I shall be happy to negotiate/I am sorry but I cannot consider leasing to Penguin the following titles.
>
> Please delete whichever phrase is inappropriate.
> Back came the postcard with everything struck out up to and including the words 'I am sorry'.

(from *King Penguin*, J. E. Morpurgo)

Aubrey Forshaw was the head of Pan paperbacks until 1970, a large, impressive and popular figure. Unfortunately he liked to read for himself the books for which Pan was contemplating a major bid; he had a variety of outside interests, including vintage cars, and anyway was a slow reader, and his Pan colleagues' affection for him sometimes faltered.

Dwye Evans of Heinemann was persuaded to give Pan first refusal on *The Godfather*, and Clarence Paget, then Editorial Director, instantly saw the book as a bargain to be snapped up. Forshaw was less convinced: 'It's a dirty, big American book, and they always fail. But I'll read it.'

The Godfather is indeed a big book, and after three days, when Dwye Evans genially asked what the decision was, Forshaw had read thirty pages.

The days lengthened into weeks, Forshaw slowly read on, and Evans's geniality diminished since he was being pursued by other paperback publishers desperately eager for the book. Finally, his patience snapped. He rang up early and icily told the Pan editors, 'It is now three weeks; if you don't make a good offer by one o'clock today, *The Godfather* goes elsewhere.'

Forshaw arrived at about 11 a.m. and was – with some vigour – apprised of the extreme urgency of the situation.

'Oh dear,' he said, 'I'm afraid I can't make a decision this morning.'

'Why not?'

'Well,' he said, 'I've arranged to have a haircut.'

At that point the Pan management exploded. They cancelled the haircut, summoned a taxi and accompanied Forshaw to the Heinemann offices where the deal was concluded. Back at Pan, Aubrey Forshaw looked round benignly.

'That,' he said comfortably, 'was a good bit of business. I always *knew* we wanted that book.'

'*Sometimes I get the piles confused . . .*'

Lord Thomson was talking about the publishing firms he had bought.

'I got these little publishers,' he mused (he had in fact bought four or five quite large companies), 'and now they send me a lot of books to read.'

'Do you read them all?'

'Indeed I do,' he said with just a trace of indignation. 'I have this system, see; the books I've read on the right-hand pile, the books I've not read on the left-hand pile.'

He added, with the simplicity of a very powerful man, 'Of course, sometimes I get the piles confused and then I read some goddam books twice.'

It is perhaps unfair that George Weidenfeld should feature under Sloth since he has boundless energy. A pre-War refugee from Vienna, he set up Weidenfeld & Nicolson in 1949; he published prodigously and came to know an enormous number of people.

Lord George was persuaded to hold a party to mark the retirement of John Cowan, for many years Weidenfeld's diligent Scottish representative. Directors, staff and other reps were present, including Walter Ayling, the West Country traveller. George had done his homework on Cowan's long and loyal service – but not quite well enough: striding across the room he seized the startled Walter Ayling by the hand and said, very sincerely, 'Well, John, this is a sad day for us all; I don't know what we'll do without you.'

A visitor once surprised Harry Batsford in his office. He was dictating to his secretary on one side of his desk. On the desk were his legs, encased in serviceable but unappealing long-johns. On the other side another Batsford lady was plying her needle.

Batsford deigned an explanation: 'It's my trousers, you see. They needed some fly buttons.'

There is the tale, doubtless apocryphal, of the genial Ian Parsons of Chatto and Windus showing a visitor around the King William IV Street offices in London.

'What's through that door?' asked the visitor.

'Do you know,' said Ian, 'I've never been through there. Let's find out.' He opened the door. It was the warehouse.

A similar story is attached to the firm of Scribners in Fifth Avenue, New York. It concerns the patriarchal Charles Scribner, and was told by Roger Burlingame in *Of Making Many Books*:

> C.S.'s effort to know his people by name was not wholly successful. Once when he was prowling in the cellar – the place where disgruntled authors say publishers hide their books – with a guide, he got talking to a man pushing a truck. When the man left, C.S. said to the guide:
>
> 'Who is that man?'
>
> The guide told him. 'He's been here twenty-six years.'
>
> 'My God!' said C.S. 'Longer than I.'
>
> But as they got into the elevator, the warehouseman tugged at the guide's sleeve.
>
> 'Who is that?' he said. 'Has he been here long?'
>
> 'Quite a while,' the guide whispered. 'His name is Charles Scribner.'

Teddy Cole founded a firm called Paperback Distributors over twenty-five years ago. It was an early attempt to put paperbacks into all sorts of new outlets; it failed and Cole went bankrupt for almost half a million pounds (way over two million pounds in today's values) but continued to live in a palatial house and to attend the Official Receivers' proceedings in a large Rolls.

Questioned about this apparent contradiction he replied with the utmost cheerfulness:

'My wife is doing for me what I have long done for her. She is keeping me.'

Bookselling, like publishing, has its share of agreeable eccentrics. Ian Norrie records that one such owned the Flask Bookshop, in Hampstead, during the early 1960s. His name was Fry. One day, in his window, Norrie noticed a copy of Park's *History of Hampstead* – a rare item from the early nineteenth century – for which he had an anxious customer. The shop was closed so Norrie sent a postcard asking for a quote. There was no reply. Norrie sent another. Still no answer. Several times he called at the shop but it was always closed.

One day he was tipped off that Fry was open for business. He raced round to Flask Walk and got inside before the door could be locked. There was Park, still in the window.

'How much is it?' Norrie asked. 'I don't expect any discount; I have a customer who is frantic for it.'

Fry looked miserable, muttered apologies for not answering enquiries, and then made it clear he wouldn't sell it.

'It would,' he said, 'be so difficult to replace.'

ENVY

As these pages show, publishers and other book people range pretty freely through the major sins. But they seem curiously deficient in Envy.

This is indeed odd. Publishers are surely as covetous of their neighbour's oxen, asses and chattels as other reasonable folk: they are just not envious of each other's books (they simply copy them). This situation – whether caused by clear-eyed nobility or blind vanity – left us with a nasty shortfall in this section.

Happily, however, publishers are inveterate gossips and are extremely malicious. Malice is first cousin to Envy, and anyway this is the age of the merger and the conglomerate. So we have merged the two into one single, thumping Sin.

A publisher who had published many earlier accounts of attempts at climbing the world's highest mountain was heard, on the publication of Sir John Hunt's *The Ascent of Everest*, to complain in the Garrick Club:

'It must have cost Hodders £10 a foot to get to the top of Everest.'

A minor, subtle art exists in rejecting unwanted manuscripts. Dr Johnson appears to have been an early master:

> Your manuscript is both good and original; but the part that is good is not original, and the part that is original is not good.

Voltaire (one of several to whom this story is attributed) was even more direct:

> Sir. I am sitting in the smallest room in the house. I have your manuscript before me. Soon it will be behind me.

Sir Basil Blackwell recalled a delicate rejection note from a Chinese publisher:

> We read your manuscript with boundless delight. By the sacred ashes of our ancestors, we swear that we have never dipped into a book of such overwhelming mastery. If we were to publish this book it would be impossible in the future to issue any book of a lower standard. As it is unthinkable that within the next ten thousand years we shall find its equal, we are, to our great regret, compelled to return this divine work, and beg you a thousand times to forgive our action.

At the other extreme is Sir George Alexander's rejection of an unwanted play:

> My dear Sir,
>   I have read your manuscript. Oh, my dear Sir.
>   Yours sincerely.

Occasionally authors have an opportunity of answering back, in public. On 7 October 1932, at the ninth annual guest night dinner of the Book Publishers' Representatives Association, the President read out the following letter from J. B. Priestley:

Dear Munro,

I am dictating this from my bed, where I am very busy with gastric flu. It is a very great disappointment indeed to me that I cannot be with you at your dinner. There are several reasons for this. The first is that I know I should enjoy myself in your company; the second is that I have a very friendly feeling for your Association; and the third reason is that I was looking forward to making a very artful and malicious speech. In this speech – which should now be reckoned among the lost masterpieces – I should begin by pointing out that in the whole world of books there are only two sets of people who do any real work: these are first the authors, who write the books; and secondly, the publishers' representatives, who try to sell the books to the booksellers. All the other people in this trade merely make a more or less elaborate pretence of working. The publishers themselves practically do no real work at all, if we exclude their digestive systems, which are always working at full pressure owing to the fact that they are always lunching and dining out and doing themselves extremely well. I have caught publishers doing all kinds of things – and I am afraid I cannot specify even the most innocent of them – but I have never caught a publisher working. They leave that to their travellers, that noble and industrious race of men. As for the people at the other end of the trade, the booksellers, nobody would for a moment pretend that they do any real work. I have heard them grumble about many things – for they are great grumblers – but I have never heard even them grumble because they had work to do. Their chief cause of complaint is that they lose money, but it is very easy and requires no industry to lose money. Their chief characteristic is, I suspect, a kind of inertia, which is their great weapon of defence against the repeated attacks of the publishers' representatives.

All this and a great deal more on the same subject I would have said in my speech, catching the eye from time to time of the wretched publishers and booksellers present, who, though probably far gone in liquor at the time, would yet feel a deep sense of shame. And now all these pleasures are denied me, my dear Munro, and all I can do is to say again how disappointed I am, and to wish you and your Association the best of luck.

Sincerely yours,
J. B. Priestley.

(from Representative Majority, Arthur Thrush)

Literary agents have author problems, too.

A. D. Peters were Evelyn Waugh's agents. On one occasion the Norwegian publishers to whom they were selling the rights in one of Waugh's novels returned the completed contract together with a questionnaire about the author. Would A. D. Peters ask him to complete it? It would help the Norwegian sales.

The agents sent Waugh the form. When it was returned to A. D. Peters it seemed at first that the author had completed it with the greatest correctness. Until, that is, the last enquiry – Hobbies?

To which Waugh had responded: 'Tattooing snakes on sailors' bottoms.' The questionnaire was not, alas, returned to Norway.

If publishers suffer from authors (as well as vice versa) they are also stretched by their customers. Bennett Cerf, founder of Random House, New York, went in 1935 to sell to the buyer for the large American News Company a sizeable quantity of his company's first big trade publication, James Joyce's *Ulysses*. Cerf reported what followed.

The buyer said: 'Oh, I suppose it's that dirty book *Ulysses*. I don't think it's for us.'

I said, 'What do you mean, dirty? It's all been cleared by the court.'

'Well, it's not really our kind of thing,' he insisted. 'But you're nice fellows, we'll help you a little bit. We'll take two hundred and fifty copies.' This was for the whole country, of course! So I started screaming. I got him up from two fifty to five hundred; then, after some more screaming, he made it a thousand. Then, after considerably more battling, I pushed him up to twenty-five hundred, and finally, wringing wet with perspiration, I got him up through several stages to five thousand. He had started at two hundred and fifty! Williams said, 'Well, are you satisfied?'

I felt very proud of myself, and said, 'Yes, at last you've given me the right order.'

He opened a drawer and handed me a typewritten order, made out before I came, for five thousand copies! He said, 'I thought I'd make you work for it.'

91

Authors, too, can manipulate publishers. Bennett Cerf records in *At Random*:

> The very last time we were with Faulkner was at '21' in 1962. It was then that he talked to me about Albert Erskine. Faulkner said, 'You know, I think Albert is the best book editor I know.' I said, 'Golly, Bill, coming from William Faulkner that's quite an encomium. Have you told Albert?' He paused for a minute, then said, 'No, I haven't. Bennett, when I've got a horse that's running good, I don't stop to give him some sugar.'

Victor Gollancz had a practice, at once impressive and tiresome, of making precise appointments far in advance of the event. He received a come-uppance from a distinguished American publisher to whom he proposed a luncheon engagement several months ahead. 'I'm so sorry, Victor,' said the American courteously, 'but I have to go to a funeral on that day.'

W. G. Taylor, Chairman of J. M. Dent for many years, was an exact contemporary of Sir Stanley Unwin. Both gave distinguished service to the trade and for many years were friendly enemies (or inimical friends). They played crib together. But whereas Sir Stanley's good health was notorious – he was still bounding across tennis courts in his seventies – Taylor was a lifelong haemophiliac, a poor life insurance risk indeed. It is said that when the news of Sir Stanley's death was brought to Taylor, a smile of rare and perfect beatitude spread over his face.

In the early 1950s Charles Furth, then a director of Allen & Unwin, was in New York purchasing rights from American publishers. On a visit to the Viking Press, he argued with Harold Guinzburg about a particular title for which he wanted continental rights.

Guinzburg was reluctant to give up the Continent because, as he said, 'We have Ben Russak representing us there and we feel we should hold that market.'

Furth responded: 'Russak is very active but he only visits the capital cities. On the other hand, Sir Stanley Unwin has just come back from Spain where he visited all the fishing villages.'

'Why don't we divide the market, then?' said Guinzburg. 'You take the fishing villages and we'll take the capital cities.'

Victor Weybright, when running the American office of Penguin, discovered that paperback books were not invariably seen as *books*. He explained in *The Making of a Publisher*:

> In July 1946, when George Bernard Shaw's ninetieth birthday was celebrated under the leadership of the Dodd, Mead Company, Shaw's American publisher, we issued three Shaw plays, at twenty-five cents each, under direct licence from Shaw through Penguin in England. When I told Howard Lewis of Dodd, Mead that I thought we should be in on the grand celebration which was to take place at the Waldorf Astoria, he looked at our paperbound editions of *Saint Joan*, *Pygmalion* and *Major Barbara* and suggested that we have our own party at the Automat.

Sir William Collins, discussing the Companion Guides, was asked, 'Why is the *Tuscany* volume so inferior?' 'The author died,' he said (entirely failing in his effort not to sound condemnatory) 'before he could finish it.'

A variation on this story is the report that, when told of the death at the advanced age of over ninety of a long-standing Collins author, Sir William's only comment was 'After all we've done for her?'

Later he mentioned a Collins employee who, although never satisfactory, had stayed with the firm a long time: 'He wasn't quite right for us,' mused Sir William, 'but he bowled a very useful left arm googly.'

In 1981, the Prime Minister of New Zealand, Robert ('Piggy') Muldoon was the guest of honour at a conference breakfast of the NZ Booksellers Association, in Nelson. In the question and answer session that followed his address, a hostile bookseller attacked: 'Mr Muldoon, what do you say about this talk of your introducing a tax on books?'

Muldoon considered for a moment. 'Good idea,' he said warmly, turning to an aide. 'Make a note of it.'

It was a very hot day in the 1950s. Young Mr Paul Hamlyn (now with over seventy million pounds but less affluent then) went in to sell some books to W.H. Smith's buyer, Jimmy Cruse: he was cool and immaculate in a silk shirt and elegant slacks. No jacket. Mr Cruse went to his window and looked out at the shimmering heat of Portugal Street. Paul Hamlyn asked what he was doing: Mr Cruse turned on him with a look of profound distaste, straightened his waistcoat and said, 'Looking for your bloody barrow.'

Cool and immaculate . . .

Ralph Vernon-Hunt frequently found working with Aubrey Forshaw, who was Managing Director of Pan Books from 1953–70 and died in 1981, an absolute delight:

> One evening in the late 1950s (when I was Sales Director at Pan), frustrated because I could not get a decision from Aubrey on a matter I considered to be urgent and of great importance, I sent him a personal note.
>
> Not only was it over-long, but in parts unfair, and ill-mannered to the point of outright rudeness. I re-read it and after some (minor) soul-searching decided to send it.
>
> The reply, which I received about a week later, was quite explicit:

> 'Many thanks for your note. May I recommend you a good taxidermist?
> > Yours affec.,
> > Aubrey.'

Bill Mackarell, then Managing Director of Cassell, Australia, travelled to London to be interviewed for the top job at the Australian subsidiary of Associated Book Publishers. He was successful and his new boss, Michael Turner, took him to lunch at the Garrick Club.

After a drink in the bar they were descending the broad staircase down to the Coffee Room. Bill looked round at the noble theatrical portraits lining the walls, at David Garrick's chair, at the urn reputedly fashioned from a piece of Shakespeare's mulberry tree. 'Well, Michael,' he remarked appreciatively, 'there isn't much wrong with this place that a few poker machines wouldn't put right.'

BEING FOUND OUT

This section reinforces a familiar message: presidents, publishers, printers, writers alike, all can be Found Out.

Sir Basil Blackwell retained an astonishing ease and fluency of speech even in old age, but his memory inevitably failed a little. On one occasion he made a deft and charming speech at a farewell occasion for a senior Blackwell employee on his retirement. Only a few moments before he rose to speak he had pointed to the subject of his eulogy and said, 'Who's that feller? Never seen him before. Don't like the look of him.'

He recollected a publisher's representative who, eager to improve himself, was assiduously reading collections and anthologies of classical writers. 'Mr Blackwell,' he confided, 'can you help me? I can't find out about this author, though he seems to have written a lot. Name's Ibid.'

A few authors become publishing industries in their own right, Edgar Wallace and Enid Blyton among them. Another was Alexandre Dumas who, unlike Wallace and Blyton, employed a team of 'ghosts'. Once Dumas met a friend in the street. Dumas enquired:

'Have you read my new novel?'

'No. Have you?'

Authors tend to prefer their publishers to look like publishers, but then this story concerns an editor . . .

In *Portraits from Life*, Ford Madox Ford recorded his disturbing first meeting with D. H. Lawrence. Ford was editor of the *English Review* and received in 1909 from a lady admirer of Lawrence's a story called *Odour of Chrysanthemums*. Convinced that he had discovered a new genius, Ford asked the young writer to call – after subduing a feeling of panic about how he would engage the son of a coalminer in conversation. Lawrence appeared at the door, vital, foxy:

'This isn't my idea, Sir, of an editor's office.'

Utterly confused, Ford stumbled through a defence of his comfortable refuge from the world, with its harmonious proportions, Chippendale furniture and a nice view of trees through the windows.

> 'That's all very well. But it doesn't look like a place in which one would make money.'
>
> I said with the sort of pained gladness that one had to put on for that kind of speech:
>
> 'Oh, we don't make money here. We spend it.'
>
> And he answered with deep seriousness:
>
> 'That's just it. The room may be all right for your private tastes . . . which aren't mine, though that does not matter. But it isn't one to inspire confidence in creditors. Or contributors.'

Probably the greatest single problem a publisher faces is how many copies of each title he should print. If he prints far too many, the unsold copies will surely make the whole operation unprofitable; if too few, he increases his price, diminishes his profit and creates a body of cross customers and booksellers. Generally publishers seem to err in the direction of over-printing – sometimes grossly.

Andrew Chatto's large office at Chatto & Windus was, fittingly, heavily lined with books, shelf upon shelf of them. One effusive lady visitor examined them:

> Oh, Mr Chatto, she gushed, 'do you keep a copy of *every* title you publish?'
> 'Madam,' he replied heavily, 'in many cases, thousands.'

*

The American publisher Alfred Knopf liked firm sales; he hated sale or return deals. 'Sale or return,' he said grimly; 'you go to your empty warehouse and say, Gone today, here tomorrow.'

*

On a similar note, at a Granada publishing budget meeting some heated debate took place on the subject of the apportionment of warehouse overheads, as between the hardback and paperback divisions. Alewyn Birch, the Managing Director, in appreciation of the fact that most of the company's profits came from paperback sales, pronounced that the hardback division should bear warehouse costs at the rate of 11 per cent of turnover, whereas paperbacks would contribute 7 per cent.

'Wait a moment,' declared one of Birch's senior colleagues (a hardback man, naturally). 'Surely it should be the other way round: the paperbacks pass through the warehouse twice – once when they go out and once when they are returned.'

Michael Rubinstein remembers that in the 1930s an author client of his father's was caught fiddling his tax returns. He was a best-selling writer, receiving large royalties from his publishers, and the sum involved was very substantial. Rubinstein arranged to consult a leading Tax Counsel of that era, detailed accounts and instructions were delivered, and a few days later there was a conference in Lincoln's Inn.

'It could be very serious; *very* expensive at best,' the blanching author was advised, 'but I'll just have a word, unofficially of course, with a great friend of mine who's pretty high up in the Inspectorate.'

All sat spellbound throughout a long one-sided conversation, as his legal champion described our client's ghastly fraud on the Revenue and concocted a hardly credible range of misfortunes and mitigating circumstances. 'What? Who's that? Oh! Aren't I speaking to . . . Oh!' He put the 'phone down and turned to us, gulping. 'Er, it turned out I wasn't speaking to the chap I know, after all . . .'

Angry Penguins was an Australian literary magazine of some prestige in the mid 1940s; Max Harris, its co-publisher, was a well-known literary figure and became a notably enterprising and unconventional bookseller and journalist.

Harris was deeply impressed when he received a collection of sixteen poems, *The Darkening Ecliptic*, from the sister of Ern Malley, who had chanced on them after Ern's untimely death at the age of twenty-five. Harris devoted twenty pages of the magazine to the dead Ern and his works, declaring in a long eulogy, 'this unknown . . . is one of the most outstanding poets we have produced here . . . here is the perfection and integration of his poetry.'

The following is a sample of Ern's perfection and integration:

> In the year 1943
> I resigned to the living all collateral images
> Reserving to myself a man's
> Inalienable right to be sad
> At his own funeral
> (Here the peacock blinks the eyes of his
>   multipennate tail.)
>   from 'Petit Testament'

Sadly, it emerged that Ern had been created by two soldiers – who had in fact written verse in a different vein – Corporal Harold Steward and Lieut James McAuley. And the perfection and integration which Max Harris so admired had been achieved by opening at random books on a variety of subjects and joining the jumbled words and phrases into 'verse'. And hoaxing Harris.

It is an old saying among gardeners that a garden with no weeds in it usually has no flowers in it to speak of either. It is similarly paradoxical that the more successful a publishing firm is, the longer is the list of successful books they have refused to publish.

Victor Gollancz, who made his bow as an independent publisher in 1928, and in his thirty years of prime activity probably produced more 20,000-sellers than any other publisher of any period, nevertheless turned down all the following for one reason or another: *How Green was My Valley, Forever Amber, Room at the Top.* Also *Animal Farm*, as did Faber, on the advice of T. S. Eliot.

Martin Secker, who published most of D. H. Lawrence, and accumulated a list of almost legendary literary distinction between 1910 and 1935, used to speak with regret about allowing Alec Waugh's *The Loom of Youth* and Firbank's *Vainglory* to 'get away'. Both were first novels, and he recommended both authors to take them to his friend Grant Richards, who published them both, the second at the author's own expense.

Secker used to tell how, shortly after Richards had agreed to take *Vainglory*, Ronald Firbank paid another visit to Secker's office in the Adelphi on a busy Friday afternoon, stuck his head coyly round the door, announced shrilly to no one in particular, 'Grant Richards has taken my novel – so there!' – and vanished.

Tony Godwin enjoyed a meteoric career in publishing. He was for a while the undisputed whizz kid at Penguin. As he and Sir Allen Lane were both mercurial figures it was not surprising that by 1968, in Sir Robert Lusty's phrase, 'a typical Lane disenchantment was under way', and Godwin departed with an £18,000 handshake.

When in power at Penguin, Godwin's judgments were always confident, and sometimes very odd. Michael Joseph, suggesting that they might do quite well as paperbacks, sent him a proof of a first book and the typescript of a second written by an unknown Yorkshire vet under the name of James Herriot. (Pan subsequently bought the pair for a £1,000 advance.) Godwin declined the suggestion: he didn't think the vet's books would be at all saleable.

On another occasion, Gollancz sent him the forthcoming novel of quite a promising author, Penguin having published his first two books for an advance of £300 apiece. This time Godwin bid £400; Pan got the title with £1,750. The author was John Le Carré; the book, *The Spy Who Came in from the Cold*. Shortly afterwards, Pan's Editorial Director, Clarence Paget, met Godwin and apologised for having – however legally – 'pinched' a Penguin author. To which Godwin memorably replied, 'You're welcome to Le Carré – he hasn't got any future.'

✳

The late Lord Nelson, always interested in the business of books, was walking across Trafalgar Square with Miss Christina Foyle when an American tourist asked him the way to Foyle's famous bookshop.

Lord Nelson directed him, adding, 'This lady with me is, in fact, Miss Foyle herself.'

'And I suppose,' said the sceptical American, looking at the column towering above them, 'you're Lord Nelson.'

'As a matter of fact, I am.'

Presumably Beryl Bainbridge's gifts as a writer must have ensured her ultimate success. But it might have been much delayed, for Duckworth certainly mislaid the typescript of her first novel. It was the author J. G. Farrell who found it in their offices. It was propping up a table leg.

George Weidenfeld and André Deutsch are both Jewish refugees from central Europe, and both founded publishing firms in England in the 1940s which have proved lively, controversial and successful. There is an inevitable rivalry, and their relations vary from warm to lukewarm.

The great annual gathering of publishers from every part of the world takes place at the Frankfurt Book Fair every October. On one such occasion George and André were in the middle of a row of such proportions that they were not on speaking terms. Nevertheless, George came over to André's Frankfurt stand.

'Look here,' he said, 'we really can't go on with this quarrel.'

André refrained (if with difficulty) from asking, 'Why not?'

'After all,' George continued with some emotion, 'today is the Day of Atonement.'

The reconciliation was immediate: with arms around each other's shoulders they made their way to the bar to celebrate the renewed friendship and keep out Frankfurt's autumnal chill.

It was several hours later that André, seized by misgivings, hastened to a friend whom he believed to be strict in his religious observances.

'When *is* the Day of Atonement?' he asked.

His friend looked surprised: 'Why, a fortnight ago, of course . . .'

Alan Hill, hyperactive head of Heinemann in the 1970s, displayed some similarities to Sir Stanley Unwin. His remarkable skill in selling his books to foreigners the world over was not, however, always matched by delicacy as to the foreigners' feelings.

On one occasion he was some minutes late for an early evening reception in a peculiarly oil-rich Gulf state. He apologized: 'Lost my way. Went into a big smart car showroom and – would you believe it – chap was asleep on a mat on the floor. Had to shake him for a long time to wake him up.'

His host looked thoughtfully at his wrist-watch. 'Alan,' he said gently, 'he wasn't *sleeping*. He was *praying*.'

Christopher Sinclair-Stevenson of Hamish Hamilton acquired a new author. He promised to be a valuable acquisition, and Christopher determined to lavish every courtesy upon him.

Soon afterwards the author's first play was – as Christopher carefully noted – to be televised. He did not actually go the lengths of viewing it, but this did not hinder him from writing to tell the author what an excellent work it was, and how greatly he had enjoyed it.

Which was a pity: it was election time, a party political wrangle had been substituted and the play postponed for a week.

'Look here, Collins . . .'

This tale of Sir William Collins has been so widely told that there must be truth in it. He had called a publicity meeting and had roasted the publicity staff, especially the unfortunate responsible for getting titles reviewed. The *Evening Standard* had notably failed to review Collins titles.

'This,' said Sir Billy to the meeting, 'is how you do it. I shall myself talk to the *Standard*'s Literary Editor, Harold Harris.' When they were connected: 'My dear Harold, some of my people here have foolishly slipped up. Haven't been sending you some of our marvellous titles for review. I'm putting that right immediately: going to send you some of our best, latest books round in a taxi for review.'

The meeting was silent in admiration. This *was* how you did it. Sir Billy distanced the telephone from his ear and looked complacent. Then Harold Harris's voice came very clearly into the quiet room from the earpiece: 'Look here, Collins, I don't tell you how to run your fucking business. Don't tell me how to run mine.' Followed by the noise of a receiver being put down very hard.

Peter Hebdon, much liked and respected, ran Michael Joseph for over a decade until his early death in 1970. He took the notably popular author Richard Gordon to Sherratt & Hughes, the famous Manchester bookshop, for a signing session. Nobody came. They sat and waited, the manager protesting that nothing like this had happened before. 'Place was packed last week for Michaela Denis.' Time went by. 'Don't understand it. Michaela Denis did wonderfully last week. Mind you, she did have an alligator with her. . .'

Here is one bookseller's collection of howlers: it comes from Len Woodley of Adelaide.

Roger the Saurus	*(Roget's Thesaurus)*
Woodshop Manual for Ford Courting	*(Workshop Manual for Ford Cortina)*
Cases on Tarts	*(Cases on Torts)*
A Psychological Study: A Boy & His Aunt	*(A Psychological Study: A Boy & His Art)*
Hitler . . . Merry Kamp	*(Mein Kampf)*
South Africa and the Struggle for the Birthrate	*(South Africa and the Struggle for the Birthright)*
Aspects of Australian Gout	*(Aspects of Australian Government)*
Men as Women!!!	*(Men and Women)*
Catholic Protection	*(Cathodic Protection)*
About Your Herring	*(About Your Hearing)*
Atomic Abortion	*(Atomic Absorption)*
Eat Your Income Tax	*(Cut Your Income Tax)*
The Reformation Ear	*(The Reformation Era)*
Charles Mange	*(Charlemagne)*
Mad Wives' Dictionary	*(Midwives' Dictionary)*
Uses I abused in Statistics	*(Uses and Abuses of Statistics)*
Aunties in Geography Teaching	*(Arts in Geography Teaching)*

At a trade dinner Robert Maxwell made a passionate declaration against obscenity in novels, suggesting that the publishing industry should set up its own organization to censor fiction. In the question and answer session that followed, Anthony Blond rose to his feet:

'Mr Chairman, what right does Mr Maxwell have to speak on this subject? What does he know about fiction? So far as I am aware, the only fiction he reads is balance sheets.'

And finally, the archetypal story of the publisher Being Found Out.

Martin Secker, who flourished particularly in the first quarter of this century, had a deserved reputation for his dilatoriness in reading submitted manuscripts. One of his authors, who had suffered long delays from this cause, carefully gummed together all the centre pages of his latest manuscript before delivering it to Secker for approval. Many weeks passed, and the author made his way to the publisher's office.

'Have you lost my book?'

Somewhat to his own surprise, Secker quickly found the manuscript and placed it, mildly triumphant, in the author's hand. The author felt with his thumbnail.

'I don't think you even looked at it.'

'Indeed I did. Read it several times. It's just,' said Secker, 'that I'm carefully considering several significant elements in the development of the narrative.'

'You've never read it.'

'By God, I have!'

'By Gum, you haven't!'

ENTERPRISE

This final section is a short one. Indeed, purists among our readers may argue that some of these stories – since their consequences brought large financial gains – should more properly be under Avarice. But here are examples of publishers and others in the world of books showing a devotion and initiative over and above the ordinary calls of gain: it is pleasant to give this reminder that the people in this world are not all rotten to the core.

This must not go too far. Stories which in various ways show publishers as kindly, as do-gooders and Boy Scouts, have the common factor of being extremely boring. And in a book compiled to attract a wide readership and substantially to benefit a deserving cause, it would be disastrous if, at the last, charity were to creep in. . . .

The American Dream inevitably embraces the concept of the super-salesman. Carroll Merritt, head of Scribners' subscription department, told a story of such a man:

> One day Merritt got a message to report at once to C.S.'s office. C.S.'s eyes were glacial. His jaw was set and jutting.
>
> 'Mr Merritt,' he said, 'who is President of Charles Scribner's Sons?'
>
> 'Why, of course, Mr Scribner, you are.'
>
> 'Are you sure? Are you quite sure?'
>
> 'But yes . . . Why?'
>
> C.S. pointed to the telephone.
>
> 'My friend, George Spifkins,' he said, 'President of the United Pacific Coast Light and Power Company, has just called me from San Francisco. He tells me the President of Charles Scribner's Sons is sitting in his office selling him a set of Henry van Dyke.'
>
> By wire, Carroll Merritt fired the old-line salesman. But a month later, while wandering about the fifth floor, Merritt glanced into C.S.'s office and was astonished to see his ex-book agent sitting, not on a chair, but on C.S.'s desk. Furthermore, C.S. was at the desk, his face obviously working against an explosion of unprecedented laughter.
>
> 'But don't you see, Mr Scribner,' the agent was saying, 'you can't get to see a man these days unless you are on his level. Now George Spifkins is President of . . .'
>
> 'Listen to me,' he said. 'You can be Vice-President if you want. That's Arthur's job. You can even be Secretary. But you've got to let me be President – at least to my old friends.'

(from *Of Making Many Books*, Roger Burlingame)

Stanley Shaw Bond (1877–1943) the energetic and superbly professional reviver of Butterworths' fortunes was 'a sickly youth' put into that company by his father at the age of eighteen 'so that I should have a quiet and easy life. But things happened otherwise.'

His anecdote about his eagerness to engage the Earl of Halsbury as Editor in Chief of *The Laws of England* shows that the enterprising publisher has much the same instincts, whether his chosen field is popular or specialist:

> I decided I must have the support of the top men if the idea was to succeed. I determined to invite the Lord Chancellor to be Editor in Chief and I obtained an interview with him. He was obviously interested but said he must have time to think it over. I waited for a while and then, hearing nothing, I made enquiries to find, to my consternation, that Lord Halsbury had gone on holiday to Nice. As I needed to start as soon as possible, I took myself to Nice and finally ran Lord Halsbury to earth in an hotel.
>
> I accosted him in the foyer and in surprised tones he said, 'Hello Bond, what are you doing here?' I replied, 'I've come for my answer, my Lord.' 'But I'm on holiday,' Halsbury replied. 'I'm sorry, my Lord,' I said, 'but I must have a reply one way or the other.' 'Well, Bond,' he said, 'I admire you for your cheek . . . and, yes, I'll do it. Only, Bond, the labourer is worthy of his hire . . . eh?' 'Name your fee, my Lord,' I replied. He named it and it was a stiff one. I pulled out my cheque book and wrote him a cheque for the lot.
>
> 'Done, my Lord,' I said.

(from *Butterworths: History of a Publishing House,*
H. Kay Jones)

Norman Douglas wrote the last words of *South Wind* on Christmas Eve, 1916. His publisher took the lot to London on 27 December and sent it off to the printer. Though a long novel, close on one hundred thousand words, it was published less than four months later; and this although the proofs had to be sent to the Mediterranean for Douglas to correct, across a Europe in the throes of the First World War. Douglas being Douglas, no one knew exactly where he was. To be sure of catching him somewhere, duplicate copies were sent, one to each of his known Mediterranean addresses in Mentone and Viareggio; they were despatched ninety-six pages at a time on successive days so as to avoid their travelling on the same mail train. Somehow it worked.

In the 1920s, when Hemingway first came to be published in England, the sole title to publish which Jonathan Cape Ltd held at the start was a two-line letter from the author: 'Dear Cape, I understand you are to be my British publisher. Cordially yours, Ernest Hemingway.' Not a word about royalty rates, advances or rights. A wonderful way to put, and keep, a publisher on his mettle!

In fact, Cape had first met Hemingway in Paris, and continued to do so on and off at the Café Regence throughout the 1920s and 1930s – Hemingway never came to England at all before 1944. As the years went on Cape was careful to put his Hemingway arrangements on a more permanent and unassailable basis; but that is how it all started.

From time to time, an enterprising author who has finally tired of the sins of publishers decides to Do It Himself. The most notable example appears to have been Adolf Hitler. And what happened? He behaved like a publisher:

> The purchase of his big and comparatively expensive book, *Mein Kampf,* is imposed by law on a large proportion of the eighty million inhabitants of greater Germany. And Hitler, Dictator, receives a fat royalty on every copy thus forcibly sold: probably the most blatant case of corruption in high places that the world has ever seen. Marriage is encouraged by every possible means, equitable or otherwise, and married couples must, by law, buy a copy of *Mein Kampf.* There were 609,770 marriages in 1936, and 618,971 in 1937. The copies sold to them alone multiplied by Hitler's royalty make a nice sum in marks. And couples are similarly incited by every possible means to have as many little German children as possible, all of whom when they grow up and marry must in their turn buy their own copy of *Mein Kampf,* and so on and so on for ever and ever, throughout the duration of the Hitler régime, and each time a fat blob of royalty drops into the Hitlerian pocket. When he dies, as even he must one day, then the descendants, the sister housekeeper, and Alois, the pastry-cook, and, if she still holds that honourable office, perhaps Alois's Irish wife, and their putative descendants, and other obscurer members of the family who will turn up out of the East Mark, Austria, will inherit the royalties that will continue to flow in after his death, for fifty years after his death, during the legal term of copyright.

And do they, one wonders?

(from *Memoirs of a Booklegger,* Jack Kahane)

There is little about libraries in this collection, so it is pleasing to record that the British Museum Reading Room was seen by many famous authors as more than an intellectual and spiritual home.

Karl Marx appreciated its shelter and warmth as well as the incomparable collections; he was known to sit at a desk reading, his mind preoccupied with the significance of capital, his stomach rumbling from want of food. George Gissing was once so poor that upon occasions when visiting the Reading Room, he would use the soap in the lavatory to wash his socks. He was not alone in the practice. In the *Private Papers of Henry Rycroft*, the author recalled that:

> Once, on going down to the lavatory to wash my hands, I became aware of a notice newly set up above a row of basins. It ran somehow thus: 'Readers are requested to bear in mind that these basins are to be used only for casual ablutions.'

Ian Hay, the highly successful author of the 1920s and 1930s, chanced upon an Edinburgh bookseller who 'anticipated the idea of the eulogistic jacket'. He ticketed books: 'Will Make your Blood Run Faster', 'A Tear or a Smile on Every Page', 'Opens a Window on a Woman's Soul'. The ticket on Hay's latest book read: 'Very Funny'.

Ian Hay introduced himself. 'Of course,' said the bookseller defensively, 'we don't *read* the books; we write out these wee tickets to suit all tastes and put one on each.'

When next the author looked, his title had a revised ticket, evidently considered a fool-proof seller. It read encouragingly: 'By Well-Known Edinburgh Gentleman'.

The staff amenities of Hubert Wilson's shop in Ship Tavern Passage did not initially include lavatories. This resourceful bookseller placed in his shop, constantly visible from his office, a tin containing a small number of pennies: 'When it's absolutely necessary,' he said to his assistants, 'you take one and go to the conveniences across the street.'

Ian Parsons of Chatto & Windus once berated an editorial meeting that was agonizing lengthily whether to take on a risky book. 'Let's be bold,' he declared. 'Let's be really adventurous for a change . . . let's turn it down.'

Similarly wise was Jonathan Cape. In the house magazine *Now & Then* of 1930 he wrote: 'The common error is to say yes too often; no publisher ever went bankrupt because of MSS rejected.'

Graham Lord, Literary Editor of the *Sunday Express*, went to interview Monica Dickens. As he pressed her doorbell, his zip went. It went irrevocably and Miss Dickens commented on his constrained stance. When he had explained the situation she brought a sewing basket and a large bath towel; the exchange was effected and by the time the interview was over the zip had been made safe.

Miss Dickens wrote to Graham Lord the next day. She directed the letter to 'Lord of the Flies'.

Most non-fiction books need an index, and professional indexers become both ingenious and inventive. One such indexer, faced with an intractable problem in a medical textbook, side-stepped neatly:

'Diet, anus, artificial, patients with, for . . .'

It may be that the speed of Lord Weidenfeld's mind outstrips those of lesser mortals, as this tale rather suggests. He conceived the idea of commissioning a book from the doughty Labour politician, Shirley Summerskill.

'Get Shirley on the 'phone,' he instructed his secretary. 'Make a date and tell her I want to publish her autobiography.'

The date was made, the day duly arrived, but no Shirley Summerskill. Time passed. Lord George glanced out of the window.

Scurrying across the road, characteristically tardy, was Shirley. But not Summerskill. It was another left-wing politician, Shirley Williams.

To his credit, George published her.

When Stanley Unwin was married by the famous preacher, Dr R. F. Horton, in Hampstead, he seized the opportunity to 'fix up the terms for his autobiography in the vestry'.

Ralph Vernon-Hunt of Pan, the paperback publishers, and André Deutsch went to Frankfurt together by car one year. In the late evening, very tired and in pouring rain, they decided they couldn't face the journey on the Autobahn any longer, so they stopped at a *gasthaus* for the night. There was only one room available with 'the largest double bed in north Germany' according to the proprietor. Ralph and André were not worried; they fell into the bed and were both soon fast asleep.

Some two hours later Ralph was woken by a heavy dig in the ribs.

'What is it, André?' he groaned.

'Wake up, Ralph, wake up!' replied André, ever conscious of paperback sales possibilities. 'I have just thought of the *very* book for you.'

'Wake up, Ralph!'

INDEX